SAVING THE WORLD IN FIVE HUNDRED WORDS

SAVING THE WORLD IN FIVE HUNDRED WORDS

Perspectives on Nationally
Competitive Scholarships

Edited by Suzanne McCray, Craig Filar,
and Kyle Mox

The National Association of Fellowships Advisors

THE UNIVERSITY OF ARKANSAS PRESS
FAYETTEVILLE
2024

ISBN: 978-1-68226-257-3
eISBN: 978-1-61075-827-7

28 27 26 25 24 5 4 3 2 1

Manufactured in the United States of America

♾ The paper used in this publication meets the minimum requirements of the American National Standard for Permanence of Paper for Printed Library Materials Z39.48–1984.

Library of Congress Cataloging-in-Publication Data
Names: McCray, Suzanne, 1956– editor. | Filar, D. Craig, editor. | Mox, Kyle, editor. | National Association of Fellowships Advisors, issuing body.
Title: Saving the world in five hundred words : perspectives on nationally competitive scholarships / edited by Suzanne McCray, Craig Filar, Kyle Mox.
Description: Fayetteville : The University of Arkansas Press, 2024. | Includes bibliographical references and index. | Summary: "Saving the World in Five Hundred Words, a publication from the National Association of Fellowships Advisors, offers a unique set of resources for advisors negotiating the complex world of nationally competitive awards. The essays here focus on three main aspects of fellowships advising: serving students, ensuring access, and developing the profession. Essays range from practical advice on how to assist students with applications, to recommendations for recruiting a broad range of students more effectively, to innovative teaching and advising practices"—Provided by publisher.
Identifiers: LCCN 2024009763 (print) | LCCN 2024009764 (ebook) | ISBN 9781682262573 (paperback) | ISBN 9781610758277 (ebook)
Subjects: LCSH: College students—Scholarships, fellowships, etc.— United States. | Counseling in higher education—United States. | Scholarships—United States.
Classification: LCC LB2338 .S28 2024 (print) | LCC LB2338 (ebook) | DDC 378.3/40973—dc23/eng/20240403
LC record available at https://lccn.loc.gov/2024009763
LC ebook record available at https://lccn.loc.gov/2024009764

CONTENTS

Part III: Developing the Profession

ACKNOWLEDGMENTS

This volume includes many essays that resulted from presentations delivered at recent National Association of Fellowships Advisors (NAFA) conferences, including the July 2019 conference in Minneapolis, Minnesota, and the 2021 conference, which was held virtually. Events of this size and complexity require incredibly hard work from many talented people. The Minneapolis conference would not have been possible without Kyle Mox (Arizona State University), who was the president of NAFA at the time of the conference and demonstrated tremendous effort in shepherding through several key changes to our constitution and bylaws. As vice president for the two years leading up to that conference, Craig Filar (Florida State University) served as chair of the conference planning committee and was instrumental in the planning and execution of that meeting. Filar then transitioned to the role of NAFA president, at which time Cindy Schaarschmidt (Pierce College) assumed the vice presidency and took the lead for planning our 2021 conference, which was held virtually, for safety's sake during the COVID-19 pandemic.

The bulk of the credit, however, belongs to the conference planning committees, which for the 2019 conference included Rosanne Alstatt (Purdue University), Andrus Ashoo (University of Virginia), Heather Campbell (St. Olaf College), Elizabeth Colucci (University at Buffalo, State University of New York), Tim Dolan (University of Mississippi), Megan Friddle (Emory University), Jennifer Locke (Occidental College), and Ginny Walters (Minnesota State University, Mankato). We are grateful for the excellent work of local chair Meredith Wooten (who was at Drexel University at the time of the conference and is now at the University of Pennsylvania), who provided substantial support and access. Elizabeth Colucci spearheaded the New Advisors' Workshop, while Megan Friddle and Lora Seery

(Institute of International Education [IIE]) organized the Fulbright Reading Session. For the 2021 virtual conference, the conference planning committee consisted of Tony Cashman (College of the Holy Cross), Jason Ezell (Loyola University of New Orleans), Megan Friddle, Alicia Hayes (University of California, Berkeley), Beth Keithly (University of Texas, Dallas), Katya King (Williams College), Samantha Lee (University of Notre Dame), John Mateja (Goldwater Foundation), Anne Moore (Tufts University), Laura Perille (University of Denver), Leslie Pusey (who was then at the University of Tennessee, Chattanooga, and is now at James Madison University), Kelly Thornburg (University of Iowa), Daniel Villanueva (Cultural Vistas, Congress-Bundestag Youth Exchange for Young Professionals), and Jake Dawes (Atria). Some of these committee members have moved on to other colleges, foundations, or even other professions, but they left their mark on the NAFA community, helping our organization continue to move forward and persist during an incredibly challenging time in our nation's history.

As always, John Richardson (University of Louisville) continued to be an invaluable asset for NAFA, working first as treasurer (2001–13) and then as NAFA's first employee (2014–present). Additional administrative support was provided by Maya Azar in 2019 and Jake Dawes in 2021.

Other board members who contributed to the effort who have not been named elsewhere but deserve recognition include NAFA executive officers Brian Souders (University of Maryland, Baltimore County), Jeff Wing (Virginia Commonwealth University), and Lauren Tuckley (Georgetown University) for their important contributions to the site selection and planning.

The foundations, agencies, and organizations that sponsor national scholarships and fellowships are, as always, key members of NAFA, sharing their expertise with advisors at conferences, during campus visits, and in the proceedings. Special thanks to NAFA board member Sue Sharp (IIE) and to all the foundation members who participated in the structured foundation interviews or "chat" sessions. Representatives (at the time of the conference) who gave generously of their time included Sonja Arora and Gisele Muller-Parker

(National Science Foundation Graduate Research Fellowship), Derrick Bolton (Knight-Hennessy Scholarship), Jeff Cary (Boren Scholarship), Carolina Chavez and Trina Vargo (Mitchell Scholarship), Jane Curlin (Udall Scholarship), Robert Garris and Wyatt Burton (Schwarzman Scholarship), Elliot Gerson (Rhodes Scholarship), Stefanie Gruber-Silva (German Academic Exchange Service [DAAD] Scholarship), Craig Harwood (Soros Fellowship), John Holden (Yenching Academy Scholarship), Bo Knutson and Natalie Spencer (Critical Language Scholarship), Lewis Larson (James Madison Fellowship), Lauren Marquez-Viso (Rotary Scholarship), John Mateja (Goldwater Scholarship), Christine O'Brien (Ford Foundation), Patricia Scroggs (Rangel Fellowship), Lora Seery (IIE and Fulbright Program), Jaclyn Sheridan (Pickering Fellowship), Jim Smith (Gates Cambridge Scholarship), Kelsey Ullom (Gilman Scholarship), Tara Yglesias and Terry Babcock-Lumish (Truman Scholarship), and Katherine Young (Hertz Fellowship). We thank the foundations they represented for their ongoing support of NAFA.

Thanks also go to the publication and technology committee, which included Lauren Tuckley and Kelly Thornburg, who served as cochairs; Monique Borque (Willamette University); Brian Davidson (Claremont McKenna College); Laura Clippard (Middle Tennessee State University); Valerie Humas (Baruch College, City University of New York); Suzanne McCray (University of Arkansas); Liz Romig (American University); and John Richardson.

The editors also want to thank key supporters at their home institutions. At Arizona State University, thanks go to former dean of Barrett, the Honors College, Mark Jacobs; former provost Mark Searle; and President Michael Crow for supporting this work, not to mention the entire staff of the Lorraine W. Frank Office of National Scholarships Advisement, both past and present. At Florida State University, special thanks go to former president John Thrasher, President Richard McCullough, former provost Sally McRorie, Provost Jim Clark, Dean of Undergraduate Studies Joe O'Shea, and the teams of the Office of National Fellowships and the Office of Graduate Fellowships and Awards.

Thanks go as well to Charles Robinson (chancellor) and Terry Martin (provost and executive vice chancellor for academic affairs) of the University of Arkansas for their ongoing support and to the staff of Enrollment Services and the Office of Nationally Competitive Awards. Emily Wright (senior associate director), Matt Halbert (associate director), and Kathi Davidson (chief of staff) provided excellent proofreading support. William Clift designed the striking cover. The continuing support of Ketevan Mamiseishvili (dean), Michael Hevel (associate dean), and Kristin Higgins (chair of the Department of Counseling, Leadership and Research Methods) in the College of Education and Health Professions has been greatly appreciated. And of course, this publication would not be possible without the excellent work of the University of Arkansas Press: Mike Bieker (director), David Scott Cunningham (editor in chief), and Charlie Shields (marketing director).

SAVING THE WORLD IN FIVE HUNDRED WORDS

To say that much has changed in the world since the 2019 National Association of Fellowships Advisors (NAFA) conference in Minneapolis, Minnesota, is certainly an understatement. The theme of our most recent in-person conference was "the process continues," an acknowledgment of the mutable nature of our work, the ever-ongoing process of professional development required to be an effective fellowships advisor, and the necessity of *learning to learn* in the dynamic context of US higher education. We discussed best practices for diversity, equity, and inclusion; considered the dynamic context of US higher education; and interrogated several long-standing issues including definitions of central but nuanced and even controversial terms like *merit*, *excellence*, and *success*.

Little did any of those attending the conference know how important the outcomes of these discussions would become. Following the emergence of the COVID-19 pandemic in the spring of 2020, global economic, educational, public health, and political institutions irrevocably changed—in some ways for the better, some not, and some yet to be determined.

The work of fellowships advising has always been about relationships. To be effective, advisors nurture trusting relationships with applicants, administrators, faculty, award sponsors, and each other. Advisors seek assistance in recruiting competitive students to appropriate scholarships from faculty and administrators across our campuses. When those students are lucky enough to be invited to interview, advisors ask again for support during practice interviews. More support is needed when the news arrives about who has won and who will now be seeking opportunities elsewhere. Advisors facing complex situations connect with other advisors or with foundations to ask questions, to share issues, and to seek wise counsel. And any advisor who has been more than two weeks on the job immediately appreciates the importance of the face-to-face conversation, the work that happens across the desk with a student, the most important relationship of all.

So what happens when we are all sequestered at home? What happens when our campuses become vacant and our metaphorical desks are replaced by videoconference screens? Like all good advisors, we abide and we adapt. Our 2021 conference became virtual, with the quite obvious yet optimistic theme, "embracing change." The inherent dedication and imagination of our colleagues became apparent as we sought to recreate the connections that are so vital to our work through virtual workshops and breakout sessions. Although the context had changed significantly, we stayed the course, opening the event with a workshop focused on "inclusive excellence." We acknowledged that now, more than ever, stakes were high for students at the margins.

We reckoned with the impact of a global pandemic and the immediate manner in which it challenged us to reconsider and revise strategies. At the same time, we also faced a reckoning of institutional, organizational, and personal responsibility for creating inclusive and accessible spaces for our students, our offices, and our organization. The two moments entwined in such a manner that our conceived paradigms of fellowship advising were questioned in a constructive way to push NAFA and our field forward. We did this work collectively as an organization and supported one another as we worked on our individual campuses. And through it all, the motivation and the heart of our work provided a steady compass point for us in our guidance to a true north of growth and inclusive experiences. We remain committed to supporting, educating, and mentoring all students in their pursuit of excellence and impact through nationally competitive awards applications. Our commitment to our students and to one another helped us meet the challenge of the past four years and has given us the space to ask and attempt to answer difficult questions to improve the quality and the reach of our work as fellowship advisors and foundations.

Saving the World in Five Hundred Words: Perspectives on Nationally Competitive Scholarships is the ninth collection of essays produced by

NAFA in conjunction with the University of Arkansas Press. Each collection has focused, at least to some extent, on a particular topic—providing value throughout the process, supporting students who focus on the public good, advising student leaders, developing an effective advising office, and minding the gaps that occur for students, given the broader contexts that affect them. The most recent publication was devoted solely to advising students on the Truman Scholarship application. As in all the volumes before it, the overall topic in this collection is supporting students, but one of the more specific themes is expanding access—supporting effectively those who are likely to come into our offices as well as those who are not. These essays also reflect the tumultuousness of the COVID-19 years along with a sense of innovation those years have inspired.

The essays in this volume were generated (for the most part) from presentations at two NAFA biennial conferences (2019 and 2021), various summer or virtual workshops, or ideas inspired by conversations had at one of these. The essays fall into three sections. Part I, "Preparing Students," provides practical advice on how to assist students with applications, with the interviews that the lucky few may then participate in, and the advising challenges of assisting equally talented students who are not selected. Part II, "Increasing Access," focuses on including often-underserved populations in the scholarship application process by rethinking recruitment efforts that may unintentionally exclude various student groups, by revamping advising itself to make sure all students feel respected and valued, and by training all staff members to do the same. Part III, "Developing the Profession," touches on a variety of topics that affect fellowships advising—collaborative research, modes of teaching and advising, the role of graduate students, and the overall professionalization of the field.

The title for this volume is taken from chapter 1 of this collection, "Saving the World in Five Hundred Words or Less: The Truman Scholarship Policy Proposal." Here Tara Yglesias (executive deputy secretary of the Harry S. Truman Scholarship Foundation) has more to add to the previously published volume of essays entitled *Wild about Harry: Everything You Have Ever Wanted to Know about the*

Truman Scholarship. As it turns out, there is more to know. *Wild about Harry* addresses various Truman application questions individually as well as graduate school planning and the Truman finalist interview. As several advisors lamented, however, a review of the Truman Scholarship policy proposal was missing, so Yglesias is back again to provide insights into what for students can be the most challenging part of the Truman application. Her advice, as always, is delivered with wit and a wisdom developed from many years as a reviewer and as a longtime trainer for those who review as well. She provides a history of the policy proposal and its impact on the overall success of an application. Truman applicants and their advisors will want to read this essay with care, as it outlines the many ways proposals can go off the rails and provides detailed guidance on how to keep things on track.

In chapter 2, Lucy Morrison (University of Nebraska at Omaha University) and Gwen Volmar (Duke University) take on the fellowship interview. Their essay "Major Awards Interview Preparation: Campus Strategies" focuses on the interview process for four major awards: Truman, Marshall, Mitchell, and Rhodes Scholarships. The essay provides best practices for preparing students for interviews based on a survey conducted with members of NAFA, a thorough review of foundation materials, and interviews conducted with foundation representatives. The background information about the interview practices of the four foundations will be particularly helpful to new advisors, for staff training efforts, and for a quick reference guide when advising students. The authors provide data on what advisors are currently doing across a variety of institution types, which may encourage new habits for even the most experienced advisor.

In chapter 3 Gregory A. Llacer (Harvard University) writes about the toughest kind of preparation that advisors do—consoling exemplary students who receive the difficult news that they have not been selected. In "What Did I Do Wrong? Counseling the Unsuccessful Fellowship Applicant," Llacer addresses how advisors can have meaningful conversations with students who do not receive a particular award. Students ask the question, "What did I do wrong?" for a variety of reasons. Some ask in disbelief, as a kind of "How is this possible?" question. Some think if they can pin down exactly where they went wrong, they can correct it and then be successful the next time. Others ask in order to make sense of their overall competitiveness.

Some scholarships provide feedback, but even that feedback can be vague. When it is specific, it can be helpful, but sometimes, as with the National Science Foundation Graduate Research Fellowship, reviewer feedback can even be contradictory. And as many foundation representatives have said, the number selected is low; the number of qualified students is high. So we are back to the "worthy many and the lucky few." But just sharing that, as Llacer points out, may not help a student who is grappling with a rejection that can feel very personal and undermine the student's sense of self. Llacer provides guiding questions that will assist advisors in helping students be more reflective about their applications and the world of highly competitive awards as well as give them a sense of resilience as they move forward with other applications, encouraging them to think of the many other options for success.

Part II looks at increasing access from various perspectives. In chapter 4, "Community College and Transfer Student Access to Nationally Competitive Awards," Cassidy Alvarado (Loyola Marymount University) looks at this too often overlooked population. Alvarado conducted a study using a mixed-methods approach (interviews at a four-year college, a survey at a community college) with students who had transferred and with those who were about to transfer, to determine what their understanding of nationally competitive awards was, focusing the attention on awards— Gilman, Fulbright English Teaching Assistant, Jack Kent Cooke, and Truman Scholarships—that could be a good fit for transfer students. Alvarado reminds advisors that transfer students represent a diverse and accomplished demographic, so all who are looking to broaden the range of students put forward for nationally competitive awards would do well to recruit students from this population in a more systematic way, building partnerships with community colleges in order to start the recruitment process early and to increase awareness of and dispel any misconceptions about such opportunities.

The next three essays in this section look at ways that offices can reach a broader group of students, including those who have historically been underrecruited and underserved. Too often when students from underserved communities have been included in the competitive awards process, they have been poorly served. In chapter 5, "Exploring Diversity, Equity, and Inclusion Issues for Scholarship Offices: A Personal Journey," Karen Weber shares her experiences at Duke University as she has grown in her own understanding of the barriers many students face in applying for awards and the ways her office (and by extension other offices) can mitigate those challenges. Weber and her team have reviewed their office extensively with an eye to practices that might discourage talented students from engaging in the process. They have taken a holistic approach that has included reading relevant literature as a team, changing communications and outreach practices, and becoming actively engaged in racial and social equity efforts on their campus. Weber provides questions that awards offices can use to assess their own practices and to provide more broadly welcoming outreach and service to students throughout the process.

In chapter 6, "Connecting and Supporting Historically Marginalized Students: Access, Opportunity, and Empowerment," Elizabeth Rotolo (Brandeis University) discusses the approach she has taken at her institution to work toward culturally responsive advising. Like Weber, she provides key questions that advising offices should be asking as they conduct audits of their recruitment and advising practices. What do the messaging, space, and process communicate to students? Rotolo makes clear that the work does not end after a single review even if an office makes significant changes to adapt its messaging and practices to underserved communities, because language and student identities are complex and evolving, making improving accessibility an ongoing process.

In chapter 7, "Toward an Antiracist Fellowships Advising Model," Kurt Davies (New York University) adds to this discussion by providing a framework for understanding the systemic racism that can affect the work advisors do. Davies points to issues associated with merit selection processes both in selective college admissions and in the world of nationally competitive awards (perhaps the highest form of academic selectivity). Merit is very often inextricably tied to privilege, and opening doors beyond privilege is an important goal for most foundations and fellowships advisors. Davies supports a broad holistic review process for institutions that are selecting students to nominate that includes a broadly diverse group of candidates. As part of the selection process for awards at New York University, he has created the Application Development Cohort, a diverse group of applicants who work together in the summer to share their narratives and in turn benefit from feedback that resonates from their peers. Through this program, Davies "decenters" the fellowships advisor in an effort to have students hear from a broader group of voices, liberating their own voices in a way that may be difficult for one advisor to do.

The essays in Part II are an excellent place to start for any office reviewing its approach to broadening opportunities for underserved communities on its campus. Part III looks at additional ways that the profession is developing through research, course offerings, and graduate student advising. In chapter 8, "Zero Searches Found. Try Again? The Journey of a Fellowships Research Collective," Catherine Salgado (Arizona State University) provides an engaging look at four fellowships advisors (and also graduate students) who formed a collaborative research group. Not only did they delve into compelling research, but they also found support from others in a similar position—full-time job, part-time graduate study, and a commitment to research (as well as a life outside all three somewhere in the mix). The group settled on research about letters of recommendation and worked to provide a data-driven understanding of letters written for the Truman Scholarship. After ten months of intense, collaborative work, they were ready to submit but then faced the vagaries that often follow submissions for publication—a misunderstanding of the work or the authors or both, or a need to regroup and revise. Salgado indicates the collective did just that. They narrowed the focus to Truman academic letters and soon discovered rhetorical patterns that could be helpful for all recommenders or endorsers as they review their own letters. But the essay is about more than what hedge words a recommender uses or how a writer establishes authority and so asserts the right to discuss work or activities they have not witnessed. The essay is at its heart about the value of collaborative research to the researchers that goes beyond the facts revealed. This is truly a story of a journey toward both understanding and community.

In chapter 9, "Beyond the Pandemic: Harnessing Insights from Bichronous Online Teaching to Inform Fellowships Advising," Richelle Bernazzoli (Carnegie Mellon) and Meredith Raucher Sisson (Virginia Commonwealth University) share teaching and advising lessons learned from the switch to remote learning during COVID-19. Both adopted new methods of encouraging student engagement in the application process that they continue to employ even though face-to-face options are easily available. Introducing what for many will be a new word for mixed-mode delivery—*bichronous delivery*—if not a new concept, the authors discuss how this approach can assist small and large offices alike in creating a broader audience for and deeper engagement in information meetings, writing workshops, and application courses.

Bichronous teaching and advising (including both synchronous and asynchronous modes) offer advisors a way to invite panel participants from all over the world, actively engage students (not just inform them) through learning management systems, and conduct interactive writing workshops on software programs like Google Jamboard, all while doing so in an accessible format that reaches students on and off the campus. But as the authors make clear, advisors will need to be intentional and creative when using these tools—simply moving meetings to Zoom and conducting courses online that were designed to be face-to-face will not prove successful.

In chapter 10, Matthew Klopfenstein (University of South Carolina) closes the volume with his essay "Fellowships in Support of Graduate Professionalization." It is appropriate to end this collection with an essay about graduate advising, as that specific area has recently become its own branch within the fellowships advising world. NAFA now has a separate listserv for those who mainly or exclusively advise graduate students as opposed to advisors who work for the most part with undergraduates as they plan to do graduate work, and there are special sessions now at conferences for graduate advisors. Additionally, in the future, we anticipate that more essays will be included in the proceedings that focus on this work. Klopfenstein's essay focuses on the professional development aspect that advisors of graduate students provide. Singling out this aspect adds another layer of value for would-be partners. As an example, the author discusses the new Graduate Student Resources Hub, or Grad Hub, at the University of South Carolina as a model. Through the Grad Hub, Klopfenstein connects regularly with the graduate school and the career center in space that is identified for graduate student programming. These campus partnerships have inspired Klopfenstein to think about opportunities for NAFA to also partner with national organizations that will expand its voice and influence on the future of graduate education.

Whether advising graduate or undergraduate students, online or in person, at a research university or a comprehensive one, fellowships advisors share a desire to serve their students well, and they have good reason. Each of our campuses has students who have compiled stellar academic records and amazing lists of accomplishments; who, as Harry S. Truman famously put it, lead by "getting other people to do what they don't want to do, and like it";[1] who have genuine hearts for service; and many who themselves come from underserved communities. We admire these students and want to bring our best game to the advising table for them as they apply for awards that will help launch them on a path to change their communities, their states, their country, or even the world. We hope, regardless of scholarship outcomes, that this worthy many will find ways to realize their goals.

Notes

1. Quoted in *Wild about Harry: Everything You Have Ever Wanted to Know about the Truman Scholarship* (Fayetteville: University of Arkansas Press, 2021), 60.

PART I

Preparing Students

1

Saving the World in Five Hundred Words or Less

The Truman Scholarship Policy Proposal

TARA YGLESIAS

S ome years back, when website analytics was more a programmer party trick than Skynet trying to sell its wares, the Truman Foundation thought it would be interesting to figure out exactly when the Truman Scholarship application broke people. The method was slightly unsophisticated, but we asked for a report on when someone exited the website—basically the moment they said "nope" and closed the window to go do something else. For the vast majority of people, it was after learning about the policy proposal.

Unscientific or no, this information dovetails with anecdotal evidence from applicants and advisors. Potential applicants are surprisingly undaunted by the prospect of distilling their undergraduate careers into a handful of activities or reducing their life goals to a few sentences. They do not even mind finding letters of effusive praise and seeking a sometimes-elusive institutional nomination. But the minute we outline the policy proposal, they turn away in droves. This issue is more acute at newer institutions and with applicants who lack a policy background. For actual applicants, question 14 may be the most terrifying,[1] but for potential applicants, nothing is more off-putting than the policy proposal.

In some cases, that may be a feature, not a bug. If students have no desire to engage in policy work or discussion, they are not likely to be the sort of candidate we are seeking. The policy proposal, however, should not be a barrier simply because applicants lack (or perceive they lack) a policy background—or because we have historically not done the best job of explaining what we want to see. In this essay, I will examine the rationale behind the policy proposal, explain how it is used in the competition, and provide guidance for helping students select a topic for and develop their proposals.

History of the World, Part I

The policy proposal is the signature feature of the Truman application. In the beginning, the policy proposal was used as a litmus test. Successful applicants "instinctively" knew how to write the proposal correctly—either because their school could advise them on how to do so or because they came from a policy background. These same applicants could also easily endure twenty minutes of questions on the policy proposal alone, either because of their expertise or thanks to preparation from their school.[2] Regardless of the reason, these students were who we sought and who we felt were likely to be successful in public service. But once we began seeking a broader range of applicants from a more diverse set of institutions, the foundation realized our litmus test was more of an unnecessary ordeal.

We began to de-emphasize the role of the policy proposal in the selection process—both to our applicants and to our selectors. Students from a broader range of experiences and disciplines were able to apply, and that variety better reflected the future of public service. This change was also a recognition that with a broader pool of applicants, we would never be able to have panelists able to cover every topic with the same level of detail.[3] Our panelists were then able to engage with finalists on a broader range of topics even though the interview was often shorter.

That change allowed us to return to the original intent behind the policy proposal. We envisioned this as an exercise in both education and persuasion. The idea for the policy proposal came from the shared experience of any Washington, DC, policy wonk—trying to convince someone with power to do what is best (a subjective measure, to be sure) on a given issue. The original iteration was explicitly aimed at Congress or the executive branch—how would a policy writer convince a sitting member or subcabinet secretary to do "the right thing"? As the foundation's vision of Truman Scholars changed, so did the audience—we went from Washington, DC, to mayors' offices, to town councils, to UN committees, and to everything in between. While there might be nuances to addressing each of these audiences, the core experience remains the same—the applicant has five hundred words to save the world.

The Weight of the World

Soliciting candidates from a wider range of interests and experience with policy work is meaningless if the foundation fails to adjust how the policy proposal is evaluated. We no longer use the policy proposal as a test to see who speaks the secret language of policy. Instead, we are looking for further insight into how the applicant views power and understands the nuances of their selected issue. Applications are first read by the finalist selection committee.[4] The policy proposal is read at the end of the application, after question 14 but before the reader reviews the transcript and letters of recommendation. The policy proposal is not scored individually[5] but rather as part of these components:

- *Appropriateness for graduate study:* The policy proposal is considered, along with (deep breath) the transcript, letters, and questions 3, 6, 10, 11, 12, and 13, as part of the applicant's overall case for graduate school (to review a copy of these questions, go to https://www.truman.gov/apply/advice-guidance/sample-application-materials). For the vast majority of applicants, a well-written policy proposal that uses relevant data will be enough to make the case for graduate school. This section is scored out of three points.
- *Quality of application:* This section measures "consistency of responses, quality of writing, good picture of the candidate and their motivation for a career in public service" (see Truman Rating Form). While the policy proposal is not specifically mentioned, those five hundred words mark the

longest section of uninterrupted writing in the entire application. The Truman is not a writing scholarship, but clarity and brevity of expression are important characteristics to display. Policy proposals that are overly long, verbose, or poorly written are likely to cause issues in this metric. This section is scored out of two points.

- *Policy proposal reveals understanding of a significant problem in candidate's intended field and some ability to analyze a complex topic:* This criterion is listed as part of "essential characteristics for advancement." We are looking for applicants who demonstrate competence in this area rather than mastery (note the subtle use of "some ability"). The vast majority of policy proposals clear this hurdle. This section is a yes/no selection.

The policy proposal plays a somewhat minor role in the determination of whether an applicant becomes a finalist. Most readers spend very little time on the policy proposal, as in most cases it is only confirming attributes shown in the rest of the application. Even if it is obvious, it bears repeating: a strong policy proposal will not cause a weak application to advance, just as a weak policy proposal will not prevent a strong application from moving forward as a finalist.

But once a student is selected as a finalist, weaknesses or strengths in the policy proposal can become much more important as the application is analyzed by the regional review panel.[6] These panelists are not required to score the application (although most develop some type of ranking for the finalists they see). They are not given specific guidance on the weight or value of the policy proposal. They are told that each finalist should receive questions about their proposal, although those questions should not dominate the interview.[7]

Even with this guidance, weak policy proposals can have outsize impacts on interviews. A question early in the interview that exposes a flaw in logic can leave even a well-prepared applicant shaken. Overly broad policy proposals can sometimes expose gaps in the applicant's knowledge. Too-narrow policy proposals can leave the panel casting about for topics to discuss. Policy proposals that play it safe can leave the panel assuming a finalist lacks leadership drive. To the frustration of policy aficionados everywhere, this issue only works in the negative. A strong policy proposal will not help an applicant with an otherwise weak interview.

That is not to say flawed policy proposals are always fatal to an applicant. Many, many Truman Scholars were selected in spite of their policy proposals. But in those cases, they were able either to acknowledge the issue with their proposal during the interview and move on or to successfully pivot to another area without becoming too fixated on the issue with their proposal. In a recent example, there were two candidates on the same panel with the same (common) issue—their policy proposal assumed the federal government had authority in an area where it did not. The applicant who was not selected could not seem to recover from the issue with their proposal. The Truman Scholar acknowledged what they did not know, explained the source of their confusion, and moved on to another topic. This candidate was still able to adapt an understanding of power and grasp of the policy issue to comport with new facts. That kind of mental flexibility is an important characteristic of a future public servant.

If I Ruled the World

Selecting a topic for the policy proposal may require a brief detour into another part of the application: *Question 9: Describe the problem or needs of society you want to address when you enter public service.* While question 9 and the policy proposal do not need to be on exactly the same topic, the two should be related. In the best scenario, the policy proposal is a narrower slice of the problem discussed in question 9. Sometimes limitations of research and space mean that the policy proposal is more tangentially related. The relation between question 9 and the policy proposal does not matter in terms of application scoring, but it can save applicants time if they are able to apply the same research and preparation to both areas. Regardless, the subject matter of the policy proposal should not be a surprise twist.

It may also be helpful to remind applicants that the application— while daunting and sinister—is not some Faustian bargain.

Applicants can decide to write about something that interests them now, even if they are unsure their career will be in the same field. Very, very few Truman Scholars do exactly what they say they will in the application, so we are looking more to see how applicants think about issues than to cleave them to an issue for eternity.

There are a number of other criteria to consider when selecting a topic.[8] Applicants should select topics that have the following attributes:

- *Controversial:* Substantial debate exists on what to do and there are a variety of approaches that have some level of merit.[9] Applicants will sometimes attempt to develop non-controversial policy proposals, but that risks creating the impression that the applicant lacks leadership and vision. In order to remain noncontroversial, applicants often need to select such a small slice of an issue that it becomes nearly impossible for panelists to engage meaningfully in discussion. Also keep in mind that what might be controversial on campus, in specific disciplines, or in particular geographic areas may not be controversial to the broader community represented by our selection panels.[10] In general, our panelists follow the "reasonable man" standard.[11] While they may ask questions about how to deal with unreasonable objections, they are unlikely to dwell on them.
- *Important:* The topic should be significant to some agency or constituency. There are some issues where importance is obvious—widespread environmental concerns, general issues of welfare or public health—but there are others where it might not be apparent why an applicant would focus on this issue to the exclusion of others. The finalist should be prepared to discuss why they would make their issue a priority or, if not, what they feel should be prioritized over their proposal. This discussion can become sensitive for candidates who are personally invested in their own policy. For these candidates, it might be helpful to explore depersonalizing the proposal if

they are likely to have difficulty discussing competing priorities during an interview.

- *Not overwhelming:* The policy proposal is limited to five hundred words.[12] Nevertheless, applicants still try to create world peace in a space smaller than the average Cheesecake Factory menu. While we admire their ambition, the limitations to this approach are obvious. Less obvious, however, is exactly how to scope the issue so it can be reasonably approached in the space provided. For some policies, the limitations might be obvious geographical or legal distinctions, but others may be less clear. In these cases, it may make sense to visit the proposed solution to see if there is a natural limiting factor.

- *Interesting to the candidate:* The critical distinction here is that the topic should be interesting to the applicant, not the readers or interviewers. An applicant enthusiastically discussing their planned changes to the Office of Management and Budget's Circular A-11 can be fascinating if the applicant's excitement is genuine. Less interesting is the applicant slogging through a topic that was selected to be provocative or assigned as a class project. Applicants should have some history with the topic that is evident through their leadership or service to this point.

- *Intellectually approachable:* Some topics are overly complex or require the applicant to master a lot of information outside their interests and capacity. Some topics may be so new or opaque that it is difficult to find relevant research. Selecting the most difficult topic possible will not impress the interviewers nearly as much as being able to thoughtfully discuss a topic that is approachable to everyone. In general, panelists will educate themselves on any topic to be able to fully participate in an interview, but the standard to which they aspire is "congressional senior staffer" not "esteemed faculty chair."

- *Tractable:* Applicants should be able to discuss their topic and develop a policy in ways that are concrete and actionable. Proposals where the primary thrust is raising awareness or conducting basic research often lack sufficient depth to generate a meaningful discussion.

Once the applicant has selected a topic, the remaining steps of developing the policy proposal can be completed in any order. Yes, public policy teaches us to refine and develop a problem statement, but that approach will not work for every issue or every applicant. Rigid adherence to the process of crafting a policy proposal is fine as an academic exercise, and it may make sense for applicants to proceed in that way, but it might be more efficient for other applicants to be creative in their approach.[13]

Problem statement: Most applicants will begin here. This section should have a clear expression of the issue an applicant plans to address with the policy as well as evidence of the problem itself. The problem should be easily expressed in one brief sentence, and that sentence should be near the top of this section (if not the very first sentence). Applicants tend to try to inject drama into the policy proposal through surprise placement of the problem statement (usually at the end of the first paragraph, thus ruining the surprise). It is neither appropriate nor feasible to wring drama from a form policy proposal. There is something to be said for making the application easy on the reader.

Proposed solution: Some applicants might find it easier to begin here, particularly if they are already familiar with a program or policy that they regard as effective. This section should include a clear explanation of the proposed solution as well as evidence of a solution's potential effectiveness. Again, it is fine to lead this section with a brief description of the change that should be made.

Major obstacles/implementation challenges: Very few applicants will start here, but it is not outside the realm of possibility, particularly for applicants dealing with very unfavorable environments for their particular policy interest. If applicants begin by anticipating an objection, they can then tailor their solution and limit the scope of the problem in a way designed to overcome the objection. All applicants should take care that they are dealing with objections in a thorough and thoughtful way. It is not enough to merely point out budget constraints or political opposition; ways to overcome these objections should be baked into an applicant's proposed solution.

All of these sections—the problem, solution, and obstacles—benefit from frequent check-ins as the other sections develop. An overly broad problem statement can be adjusted to better address objections, or a too-narrow solution can be broadened to better address an identified problem. Applicants should expect this process to be iterative; they are unlikely to end with the same components they had at the start. Beginning this process early and not being too precious about the revision process are vital to creating a successful policy proposal.

Research: All applicants will research, but some will research with an eye toward finding a clear policy and adopting it as their own. So long as the material is properly cited, there is nothing wrong with this approach. Not every problem has creative solutions, and we will not incentivize reinventing the wheel when an effective solution already exists.[14] That is not to say that creative solutions or ones that applicants have developed and implemented themselves will not get their due credit, but the applicant's ability to discuss the problem, solution, and obstacles effectively is just as important.

Applicants should use persuasive research but should avoid including a laundry list of citations. Part of writing persuasively is determining which pieces of information are persuasive and which are merely nice to know. Again, return to the purpose of the policy proposal—to move the person in power to champion the applicant's proposed solution. That will be accomplished through persuasion and the effective marshaling of data, not by burying readers in a pile of references or overwhelming them with a literature review. Be aware that some reviewers will click through links, review source materials, or look up suggested reading, but just like in the real world, not every reviewer will do that. If information is critical, it needs to be contained within the page provided as part of the application.

Applicants should take care to use only reputable sources in their policy proposal. That may mean tracking down primary sources to ensure data are summarized correctly. Applicants might also want to check the source of material found on the internet. We are in an age where organizations with benign-sounding names can be anything but.[15] Again, some of the reviewers will look through the sources carefully. Any potentially biased sources are a target for scrutiny, and the applicant should be prepared to address those concerns.

Everybody Wants to Rule the World

Political considerations are an obvious component of the policy proposal, but the weight given to them has changed over the past several years. Political polarization is not just the topic of Truman policy proposals, it is a reality of our current political environment. In some scenarios, even well-reasoned policies will be opposed simply because they are being proposed by a party not in power. Supermajority legislatures and gerrymandered districts create an environment where no policy is likely to prevail.

This environment can feel very confining to applicants in some issue areas. That may mean exploring policy options at a local level if state politics are too toxic—or vice versa. It may mean adjusting a policy to make it more palatable. It also might mean trying to make the most persuasive case possible. In some extreme cases, writing the policy proposal may take on the sheen of an academic exercise. Regardless, applicants need to acknowledge the issue in the proposal itself just so precious interview time is not wasted establishing the uncooperative baseline of their local town council.

Legislative gridlock might also mean that even the act of addressing the policy proposal is fraught with peril. In general, the proposal should be addressed to the government official who has the most authority to deal with this issue. Often, that might not be the person with the most general authority; the president is very rarely the correct person to receive a policy proposal. Applicants without a background in policy or politics may need assistance in identifying the correct person to whom to address their proposal. Even with our newfound generosity around the policy side of the policy proposal, *getting the addressee right is still important.* Not only does it show a basic understanding of the topic, it also ensures an applicant will not need to listen uncomfortably when an interviewer points out that this cabinet member is not the correct person.[16] Encourage the applicant to either seek help on campus or call the office or agency they wish to address and ask if this item is within their purview.

If the office is vacant—waiting on a congressional appointment, for example—the applicant can either address it to the previous occupant of the position[17] or address the position generically.[18] Finalists should expect to be up to date on who (if anyone) occupies the position by the time of their interview and what the view of that person would likely be.

Once addressed, the policy proposal also includes a section for "issue." Please make this as precise as possible. Too many applicants just dash off something broad and generic, and it does not make the best first impression. No reader wants to get to the end of the application only to be promised a one-page proposal about "health care" or "poverty." The issue line should include a brief statement of both the problem and the proposed solution (e.g., "improving early childhood education by expanding Head Start") that allows the reviewer to appropriately calibrate their expectations.

Brave New World

With the solution developed, research done, and proposal addressed, the writing can now begin. The tone of these proposals is probably the most difficult thing to get right. Most read too much like academic papers and not enough like the elevator pitches they need to be. It might help to suggest applicants envision presenting their topics to nonprofessors.[19] Most of our panelists are not academics. We tend to have an overrepresentation of lawyers, so approaching the policy proposal like a wee dissertation is not likely to get the reaction desired.

Universities may find government relations offices to be especially helpful with tone. Likewise, university legal counsel or community relations offices can provide feedback. For applicants who lack a policy background, they can also turn to media for examples of how to frame and pitch ideas.[20] But regardless of the source, the likely message will be that successful policy proposals will be brief, specific, and understandable. No one wants a panelist to ask the dreaded clarifying question, "What do you want me to do here?"

Editing is going to be the next and most critical step. Applicants obviously need to edit for clarity and style, but they should also remember they need to hold to a word limit, even if that word limit is a bit soft. The policy proposal has a stated limit of five hundred words, exclusive of citations and prefatory material. Applicants are not penalized for going over five hundred words, unless the proposal seems very long, or the writing is very convoluted. Even then, applicants are only likely to lose a fraction of a point in the overall application quality category.

Confusingly, we also include character counts for the policy proposal, two thousand for each section, including spaces. We provided these because they are the upper limit of what can be entered into the application. Character and word counts allow for flexibility for students who may need to use longer words or technical jargon to write their proposal. We also made each section the same length to underscore that no one part of the policy proposal is more important than any other.

Applicants should not approach the policy proposal with the intention of using all the space available. They should aim to be concise and use the least space needed to convey their proposal. Again, the Truman is not a writing award.[21] Clear, concise statements are the best option for the policy proposal.

The End of the World as We Know It (and I Feel Fine)

When in doubt, applicants should return to the stated purpose of this exercise: to convince someone in power to do what applicants want done connected to their issue. Applicants should remember that the person reading their work—both in real life and as part of the exercise—is a reasonable person who wants to be helpful. They are not experts, but they are thoughtful about the policy and will raise reasonable objections. Returning to this baseline should be especially helpful for candidates from other disciplines because it should quiet the inner voice that tends to tell Truman applicants they are not doing enough. The vast majority of policy proposals are well done; the anxiety surrounding this section of the application is thankfully overblown. Whether they are familiar with policy exercises or not, all applicants come through clearly with their understanding of power and their sense of priority. Perhaps not all the applicants' suggestions are feasible, but they leave our panelists with the conviction that Truman Scholars really might be able to save the world, five hundred words at a time.

Notes

1. See Tara Yglesias, "When the Abyss Stares Back: The Eldritch Horror of the 'Additional Information' Prompt," in *Wild about Harry: Everything You Have Ever Wanted to Know about the Truman Scholarship*, ed. Suzanne McCray and Tara Yglesias (Fayetteville: University of Arkansas Press, 2021), 75–89.
2. In the 1990s, it was not unusual for successful Truman interviews to last thirty to forty-five minutes. The bulk of that time was spent discussing the policy proposal.
3. We were certainly modeling Marshall Scholarship interviews during this period. Beginning in the early 2000s, we got better about keeping time and focused instead on broader policy questions rather than means testing the minutiae of the policy proposal. Implicit in this change is the recognition that, even though it is only the difference of a year or two, college juniors are often strikingly different from the Marshall applicants they might become.
4. Our finalist selection committee is the initial committee that reviews all submitted applications and determines who is selected as a finalist. These committee members are sometimes referred to as readers.
5. A sample rating form can be found here: "Sample Rating Form," Harry S. Truman Scholarship Foundation, https://www.truman.gov/sample-rating-form.
6. Our regional review panels meet at various locations across the country, interview finalists, and select scholars. The members of this panel are sometimes referred to as panelists or interviewers.
7. The foundation endeavors to have either the executive secretary or the deputy executive secretary attend every panel. If that is not feasible for some reason, we will designate a trusted panelist to serve as the panel secretary. One of their stated roles is to prevent interviews from becoming

too narrow by, among other things, making sure the panel does not focus too much on the policy proposal.

8. Portions of this section are adapted from our website: "Policy Proposal," Harry S. Truman Scholarship Foundation, https://www.truman.gov /apply/advice-guidance/policy-proposal; as well as conversations with Suzanne McCray (University of Arkansas) and Kimberly Benard (MIT) in preparation for our 2019 National Association of Fellowships Advisors Conference presentation on the Truman policy proposal.

9. It is fine if applicants cannot see the merit in opposing approaches. They do not need to accept these other approaches but will need to be able to thoughtfully respond to the sorts of objections that might be raised by these other approaches during an interview.

10. As an example, several years ago, a finalist proposed adding a gender-neutral option to state identification documents. The material provided by the school seemed to indicate this issue was very controversial on campus, but it did not strike our panelists in the same way. The candidate came in loaded for an argument only to find a panel that was generally receptive, if slightly bored.

11. Our panels tend to have a lot of panelists trained in law schools, and we love the "reasonable person" standard. Such a person does not exist, but if they did, they would definitely use their turn signals, eat lots of vegetables, and respond thoughtfully and rationally to sensible policy recommendations.

12. We will discuss later the various controversies surrounding our word limit versus our character limit.

13. As an alumna of Maxwell's undergraduate policy studies program, I am pretty sure that paragraph amounted to heresy.

14. This stance is a corollary of our extreme dislike of an "I am going to start my own nonprofit!" response to question 12 or 13. True leadership can often take the form of implementing good ideas, not chasing vanity projects or failing to understand the landscape of available options.

15. The internet is rife with groups that sound like proper think tanks (with names that often include phrases like "Center for" or "Research" or "Institute") but are not well regarded as sources of unbiased data. That is not to say that applicants might not wish to use the data, but they should be prepared to justify why they used a potentially biased source of data or information.

16. And this can be very tricky business. For instance, freshwater fish are regulated by the Department of the Interior, but saltwater and farmed fish are regulated by the Department of Commerce. But there are exceptions

for certain lakes, fish, and types of commercial fisheries. We certainly will not expect students to instinctively know which body regulates a particular species, but we would expect them to place a phone call to find out.

17. If applicants opt for this approach, they should include a date to ensure the readers understand they are addressing someone they know to be the former occupant of the role (e.g., Secretary of Education John King, November 2016).

18. For example, "Incoming Director, Office of the Federal Duck Stamp, Department of the Interior."

19. Professors are some of my very favorite people, but they approach things differently from civilians.

20. Obviously, there are plenty of examples, and I am sure Aaron Sorkin can write such a scene in his sleep. *The Wire*, especially season 4, is the high-water mark of watching public policy fail in real time. I once recommended the *Murder, She Wrote* episode "Capitol Offense" as a G-rated way to learn about lobbying and policy on Capitol Hill. J. B. Fletcher gives a speech about abandoned canneries that is a textbook presentation of problem, evidence, solution, and obstacles. Honestly the energy of schoolteacher turned mystery-writing bon vivant probably captures what we are looking for in a policy proposal as much as anything else. This might also be a job for ChatGPT. After trying to coach it through policy proposals on various subjects, I have discovered that the one area where it excels is creating language that actually sounds appropriate for the scenario—stilted and weird but appropriate.

21. The emphasis on clarity over style is why we are probably less worried about ChatGPT than some other awards. Essentially, to have the system create an appropriate policy proposal, an applicant will have to load in so much material that they are still writing the proposal. At this stage, having ChatGPT correct the tone of writing or provide examples of policy proposals is, ethically speaking, no different from getting feedback from various carbon-based sources. Applicants will still be required to defend their choices in person, regardless of who provided them feedback.

2

Major Awards Interview Preparation

Campus Strategies

LUCY MORRISON AND GWEN VOLMAR

I nterviews are often the final hurdle before receiving a national award—and many advisors recognize that this final step can be the most tenuous in the process for both applicants and advisors. Receiving the final award rests not only on making it to the room where it happens but also on being as prepared as possible to navigate the challenges of that space. Members of the National Association of Fellowships Advisors (NAFA) work diligently to guide their students to those rooms. Indeed, many campuses publicly celebrate students attaining interviews, regardless of final outcomes, because there is a broad understanding that the interview invitation already situates the student among the best across the country. Advisors want to enable students to be their truest selves in that room, but how can advisors most support student accomplishment in such arenas? This essay outlines best practices in preparing students for success (of various kinds) in major award interview scenarios. It does so in the context of four major awards: Truman, Rhodes, Marshall, and Mitchell Scholarships. Overviews of each major award are given with respect to interview requirements; these are followed by suggestions for mock strategies at the campus level.[1]

Major award interviews can be a stressful experience for both candidates and advisors. Candidates are sometimes given notice of the composition of the interview panel and the general structure of the interview process, but individual factors vary (such as the types of exchange, the breadth or depth and style of the questioning, etc.) and cannot be predicted in advance. In addition, new advisors and advisors at institutions without a history of finalists can find it difficult to know how to assist students as they prepare for interviews, unlike those at institutions with such a history. Information for this essay was collected from advisors, foundations, and selection committee members about various aspects of the interview process in an effort to illuminate common preparation strategies, interview-day logistics, and interviewer perspectives.

The authors designed a survey in spring 2021 and then partnered with Rebekah Westphal of Yale University, who was simultaneously researching a different angle of such interview experiences. Collaboration enabled the authors to combine survey interests into one platform for respondents. The first half of the eighteen-question survey consisted of nine questions used as the basis for this essay's data.[2] The survey was distributed to members of NAFA through the NAFA listserv over the course of two and a half weeks from May to June 2021. Fifty percent of respondents completed the survey on the day it was launched; 128 total responses were received. Limited demographic information was gathered, but respondents indicated they were evenly divided between public and private institutions though student population sizes differed widely. Thirty-nine percent of respondents noted averaging one to four finalists for the award interviews under consideration, 34 percent indicated an average of five to ten interview candidates for the four awards under consideration here annually, 15 percent recorded eleven to twenty annual interview candidates, and 9 percent claimed more than twenty interview candidates annually. Some respondents did not share their candidate data or chose not to answer certain questions. While the survey was open, the authors also reached out to representatives of the Truman, Rhodes, Marshall, and Mitchell Scholarship foundations to inquire about their interview practices directly. Foundation websites also informed this discussion.

Major Awards Overview

In shaping the survey, the authors focused on the Truman, Rhodes, Marshall, and Mitchell processes, since those major awards draw candidates from across the country and do not have significant limitations on institutional access. The authors confirmed commonalities that could be helpful to new advisors preparing candidates, even while nuances for each of these awards ensure care must be taken in targeting a particular award. Given the recent COVID-19 pandemic (data gathering was undertaken in a year where remote operations dominated the major awards), it is helpful briefly to review the status of interview practices then and more recently.

The Truman Scholarships resumed in-person interview panels in spring 2023. The US Rhodes and Marshall Scholarships have traditionally brought candidates selected for interviews together in person, but both operated remotely, due to the pandemic, in 2020, 2021, and 2022.[3] However, some practices varied across international constituencies; for example, Rhodes Malaysia conducted in-person interviews in the fall of 2022. For 2024 cohorts, the US Rhodes and Marshall Scholarships resumed in-person interviews. Mitchell plans to continue to conduct interviews remotely for the foreseeable future.[4] Cost and travel time savings are significant, of course, for those interviewing remotely. Candidates (and advisors) must consider format in their interview preparation depending on the award.

They also must consider location. Truman, Rhodes, and Marshall divide student applicants by geographical region, and these awards allow candidates to choose to which region they wish to submit (either their home state or region or the state or region where they are attending college), and so advisors need to guide candidates in choosing a region. Truman invites eleven to thirteen finalists in each of seventeen regions, Rhodes invites fourteen to sixteen candidates to interview in each of sixteen districts, and Marshall accepts fifteen to twenty-three candidates for interview in each of its eight regions. Mitchell does not use a regional selection model, offering interviews to twenty finalists.

Awardee numbers are fairly consistent from year to year; sharing details about regions and finalist pools may help advisors convey to applicants both the limited availability of these awards and the level of competition should a student be selected to interview. Truman offers one scholarship for each state within each region, as well as having the possibility of recommending further regional awards (and the caveat that state awardees are not guaranteed). Rhodes selects two recipients per district, while the number of Marshall awardees varies across regions. Mitchell consistently offers twelve awards annually. Interview panel size is similar across the awards, with six being the mean (Truman has five to eight interviewers on a panel; Rhodes has seven; Marshall has four to six; and Mitchell has six to eight). Truman, Rhodes, and Mitchell have different interviewers from those who read applications, while Marshall practices differ across its regions.[5] Advisors can perhaps best prepare students for these experiences by noting commonalities across the composition of these panels, even though, of course, individuals and their approaches will vary by panel.

Panels are populated by professionals and academics, with some panels including government representatives. All the awards announce the panels' participants before the interview. Truman shares panelists' names on its website, while Rhodes and Marshall share the specific panel makeup through email with confirmed finalists. Applicants can thus know the names and titles of panelists and, to some extent, can inform themselves about interviewers' backgrounds as those might be relevant to their interactions. Advisors may need to support interviewees' understanding that some knowledge of panelists' backgrounds would be helpful in thinking through possible lines of conversation; however, too much deep diving is unlikely to be helpful and could in fact negatively affect interviewees' natural self-presentation and the flow of the interview.

Finalists need to remember that interactions are time limited. Truman interviews are twenty minutes long, while Rhodes and Marshall interviews extend to thirty minutes. Mitchell's interviews are the shortest, at fifteen minutes. Such time restrictions help advisors plan accordingly for mock interview preparation and can allow potential candidates to shape their central thoughts and remarks concisely as they think through potential questions and answers in the allotted timeframe. Connection points may be thought through ahead of the interview accordingly; for example, if an attorney is on the panel, the finalist may want to think about highlighting the legal or policy aspects of their interests as they review their application in preparation for the interview.

Final decisions tend to follow the interviews rapidly. Truman gives applicants just under a week to accept after the announcement of the awardees. Rhodes does not have a deadline for acceptance; Marshall has historically given ten to twelve days to finalists but moved to a forty-eight-hour model in 2023. Mitchell expects candidates to commit to accepting the award at the same time as accepting the interview invitation.

A further consideration for applicants is being able to attend the interview itself. Access can be a concern: Rhodes offers no financial support, while both the Truman (for hardship cases only) and Marshall foundations cover the costs of in-person attendance for finalists. When the Mitchell Scholarship interviews were in person, the Mitchell Foundation provided lodging but not support for travel. Virtual operations in recent years have increased access for some students. Many institutions, given the prestige of having a student reach the interview stage, support students' attendance at these events. Advisors should ensure that their institutions are aware of the potential costs of finalist interviews. Institutions (and advisors) need to convey to applicants what, if any, costs will be incurred by the individual applicants, since there may be applicants who do not even apply due to economic concerns.

Preparation: Standard Best Practices

Major award advisors need to remember that not all students have previous interview experience or background; indeed, for some students, an interview is a wholly alien concept. While some students may have undertaken job interviews, those could have ranged from perfunctory (first jobs working in service industries) to targeted (working on campus in a specific capacity within an office or lab environment), providing some, but limited experience. Advisors should ascertain students' familiarity with the interview format, expectations, and behaviors, being mindful of a particular institution's student body but not presuming any previous experience in interview practices. Mock interviews, discussed in depth later, are often helpful in introducing a student to interviews as a social practice, especially with respect to American cultural contexts.

Advisors often need to cross into personal territory to address other elements. Appearances have an impact, as do mannerisms, so conversations about attire, posture, and projection are vital. Students from cultural backgrounds where authority is handled differently from in the United States should be made aware of the American expectation for how such qualities as passion are displayed (raised voices acceptable in some households for conveying emphasis, for example, would be inadvisable in award interviews). There are also stark differences between in-person and virtual situations to be explored and acknowledged, although preparatory advice often straddles modalities.

For in-person interviews, students should be encouraged to look up the location of their interview and map their anticipated route ahead of time. Some may even wish to do a dry run so that there are no surprises on the day itself. Especially if students are planning to wear new shoes (not necessarily advisable), they should walk the route to the interview location ahead of time (or plan to change shoes when they get there) so that they do not find themselves with uncomfortable blisters. Awareness of time is vital: students should plan to arrive to the interview location at least fifteen to thirty minutes early, check their appearance in a mirror, and find a quiet place to settle their nerves. Students should bring nothing unnecessary with them, such as backpacks or laptops. Students should turn off their cell phones and plan to leave them outside the interview room. Many interview committees will ask that students check in with someone when they arrive. This person should be treated with the same respect and dignity as the members of the selection committee. (This seems obvious, but according to reports from foundations, it is not always so.) They may offer a glass of water or point out the restroom, but they should not be asked to run additional errands. If possible, this person should also be thanked after the interview has concluded. After entering the interview space, shaking hands with committee members may be appropriate in small groups (one to two interviewers) but can become awkward and time consuming with larger panels, especially if they are seated far away from the student. A simple verbal greeting is acceptable. Interviewers usually signal what they would prefer.

While many of these interactive aspects may seem obvious, reviewing them with candidates should help all finalists consider the many facets of the potential experience—for example, eye contact. While an interview question will be posed by a single interviewer, students should make eye contact with all the panelists while delivering the response. Special attention or gesture toward the original questioner or someone else on the committee who may have a demonstrated interest in the response is fine, but other committee members should not be ignored. Selection committees will often offer a glass or bottle of water at the start of the interview. Students can accept or reject this as they desire, but it should be noted that "interview dry mouth" can hit unexpectedly. Taking a sip of water is also a convenient tactic for buying time if students need a moment to plan their next response. If the foundation indicated it is acceptable to bring a small notebook and pen, the student may find it useful to jot down parts of a complex question. Some students may find the act of writing a keyword effective as an aid to cognitive processing.[6] Of course, virtual interviewees may find such strategies helpful as well, but should make certain it is allowable.

Other preparatory elements can be useful for both modalities. Everyone has unique mannerisms and ticks, but an awareness of the possible impact on others is important. It is essential for advisors to point out a repeated hand gesture or an inclination to utter a long "ummmm" before giving an answer. It is important to do this as early in the application process as possible so the student has time to change what may be an ingrained habit. One advantage of the virtual format is that students can record themselves in the same format as the interview to identify and work on ironing out these potentially distractive mannerisms ahead of time. Posture is significant for both in-person and virtual interviews; students should practice sitting up straight with their feet on the ground or neatly crossed. Online interviews feature the face and its appearance prominently. Working with students to ensure their faces are fully visible and accessible to interviewers is important. Students should think about minimizing background and personal distractions (excessive jewelry, themed pins or ties, etc.) and may need guidance about professional attire to understand and identify what is appropriate and also comfortable for them. Bright colors tend to show up better on camera, but garments with intricate detail can be distracting. That said, selection committees want students to present themselves in ways that reflect who they are. Giving advice about clothing may make students feel they need to buy clothes beyond their budget; advisors need to be sensitive about such concerns.

Other considerations are more relevant when preparing for virtual interviews. Cameras should be placed at eye level, with the student's face and shoulders taking up most of the screen. Students may want to ensure their virtual screen includes their hands if their gestures complement their speaking. Cameras should be pointed at a blank or simply decorated wall space to reduce distraction. Ceiling fans should be turned off. Students may wish to place a brightly colored sticker near their camera to remind themselves to look into the camera instead of at the faces of the interviewers on the screen. Students should find a quiet space where they can be alone to conduct their interview (institutions may need to provide them with an appropriate space and reliable internet service). If distractions do occur during the interview, students should be encouraged to ignore them as best as possible, since any time spent apologizing for unanticipated distractions is time not spent answering an interview question. All technology (including Wi-Fi and wireless headphones) should be charged and tested in advance in the same space that will be used on the day of the interview. Computers should remain plugged into an electrical outlet for the duration of the interview. Students also need to be prepared for the virtual interview crashing or technology failing, and they should know the steps to take if such an event occurs.

Students can also exploit the benefits of the virtual interview space. Interviewees may wish to place a comfort item just offscreen, such as a picture of someone they admire or a note with the word "Smile!"

Selection committees do not allow students to bring notes with them to the interview, however, so any such item should be for support only. Virtual interviews also merit considerations of response length. Extra caution should be taken to give responses that are concise. The virtual format makes social cues more difficult to read (e.g., interviewers are shifting in their seats or looking away; interviewers are making eye contact with each other), and as a result, students may ramble more than they would in an in-person format. They may also be less aware of their movements. Apprehension is a part of each situation, of course. Understanding the selection pools, panel structures, and operational practices of the different awards is essential for candidates as they aim for and move through these award processes; reminders of the preparatory and day-of matters reviewed here are useful for even the most seasoned interviewee (and advisor).

What the Data Show

The authors' survey aimed to ascertain what NAFA advisors do to counsel their candidates appropriately for these last award steps—and whether our cumulative knowledge could point to best (or even possible) practices across the country and different institutions. The survey's 118 total respondents indicated that when a candidate is invited to interview for a major award, the following preparation strategies are used:

- 97 percent of respondents offer one-on-one advising.
- 97 percent of respondents offer to stage a mock interview.
- 59 percent of respondents provide written materials for candidate review.
- 83 percent of respondents provide candidates with example questions drawn from previous candidates' experiences. The above 59 percent may include written lists of example questions, although other types of written materials may be reflected in that number as well.
- 35 percent of respondents offer peer advising.
- 25 percent of respondents offer interview prep workshops.

As the results indicate, the most popular responses to an invitation to interview are a one-on-one advisor meeting and the offer of a mock interview. Nearly two-thirds of all respondents provide either sample questions for candidates to review or other written materials designed to further inform candidates' preparations (such as the mock questions for finalists that the Truman Foundation provides on its website).[7] Our survey did not indicate whether interview preparatory workshops were more generally targeted at all campus applicants as opposed to those actually selected for interviews. Many advisors offer broader general workshops as part of their campus efforts in preparing students for success. Individual meetings and mock interviews are obviously regarded as the most effective interview preparatory techniques across the NAFA community.

Some advisors host interview preparatory sessions open to all applicants, all endorsed applicants, or all finalists, depending on the number of applicants and the preference of the advisor (and workload permitting). These sessions are designed to introduce students to the interview environment, including addressing many of the facets considered earlier in this essay, such as selecting appropriate attire and calming frayed nerves. Such sessions may also consider the goals of the interview, prevalent question types, and concerns that students may have in common.

Interview sessions may also be an opportunity to let new applicants learn from the experience of previous applicants. Advisors may recruit previous applicants to talk about their actual interview experience at these sessions, both because it can be an opportunity to learn practical tips from someone who has been through it before and because it allows students to see that previous successful applicants are just like them. An opportunity to mutually laugh at a blunder a candidate made (and yet still got the award!) can be very reassuring for nervous students.

Mock Interviews for Major Awards

Focusing on mock interviews and major awards, the authors' survey then drilled down further to inquire about the number, nature, and composition of mock interview panels across scholarship opportunities. Forty-one percent of advisors offer only one mock interview per candidate, 34 percent offer two, 18 percent offer three, and 7 percent offer four or more mock interviews. To staff these mock interviews, advisors invite a variety of individuals on their campuses to serve: 95 percent of advisors invite faculty to sit on mock interview committees, 70 percent utilize major award advisors, 69 percent invite other staff (41 percent of advisors invite deans or other upper-administration officials), and 65 percent ask former finalists to return to campus to join. Twenty-one percent of advisors invite graduate students to sit on mock interview committees, and 9 percent invite same-year finalists to interview each other.

Given busy and demanding schedules, arranging mock interviews is time consuming. The "ask" for participation from the campus community can be a significant one. Advisors are generally responsible for schedule coordination as well as providing sample questions to interviewers and guidance as to their roles and expectations about the mock interview itself. Given the known makeup of the national interview panels, having faculty present seems essential, since experts in the field are generally included on major award panels. Faculty are both most likely to be able to model the types and style of academically specific questions expected on such panels and most likely to be able to offer teachable and encouraging responses to students preparing for the big event itself. Similarly, inviting deans or other higher-level administrators creates a panel with administrative levels that approximate those on actual panels while also serving to highlight the success of the candidate (and their award advisor) more prominently on campus. With their experiences and investment in these processes, advisors are highly desirable as active participants on or careful observers of these mock panels.

The authors also asked advisors to share the approaches they take to the content of their mock interviews, particularly the style of interview advisors think will best prepare their candidates for the challenge of a national award interview. Most advisors (70 percent) recruit relevant disciplinary experts to sit on their mock interview panels so that the candidate can be challenged with discipline-specific questions from an informed perspective. Likewise, 85 percent of advisors deliberately prepare challenging questions for the candidate, designed as stress tests. Recognizing that there are other stressors in an interview environment as well, about 25 percent of advisors indicated that they manufacture these stressors in the mock interview to mimic some of the anxiety-provoking elements of the national interview. Such stressors include asking uninformed or confusing questions (28 percent and 20 percent, respectively), with 25 percent of advisors creating a deliberately hostile or disruptive environment in the mock interview. Only 4 percent of advisors reported creating intentional distractions (e.g., yawning, checking the time, having a phone ring) during the mock interviews. Twenty-one percent of advisors reported that they record their mock interviews so that the candidates can review their interactions with the committee.

Our survey reveals roughly 75 percent of surveyed advisors do not manufacture stressors in their mock interviews. They may find doing so adds further unnecessary challenges to what is already a stressful situation, or it may be that advisors regard the addition of such factors as untenable for the particular applicants with whom they are working. Certainly, the major award panels do not by design incorporate such stressors into their settings. Without surveying the students, we cannot assume such active stress preparation is either helpful or unhelpful; difficult questions are commonly asked, while purposeful disruptions seem to be less employed.

After national interviews are over, almost all advisors (98 percent) report that they follow up with their candidates one-on-one. The most ubiquitous practice across NAFA, such feedback is vital both for continuing to support the candidate and to inform future efforts for other candidates. Thirty-seven percent of advisors report that they ask their interviewees to write up a report about the actual interview, and thus those interviewed can help share their insights on content and context with future candidates. However, very few advisors ask former interviewees to appear at a workshop or participate in group advising subsequently (2 percent and 3 percent, respectively). Awardee status may affect such ongoing considerations, alongside time and scheduling concerns.

Mock Interviews on Campus: Tips and Tricks

Offices implement procedures differently within their mock interview structures, as the survey data revealed, but there are commonalities and specific elements to consider when undertaking these efforts. Responses across the survey questions reveal advisors recognize the delicate negotiation of the mock interview procedure for candidates: building students' confidence is desirable—but overbuilding it could be damaging. However, having a challenging or even hostile mock interview experience could be devastating for candidates, so the line between nurturing and confronting must be carefully managed by the major award advisor. A candidate experiencing negative feedback must be supported in processing such comments; for example, feedback about a hair-smoothing nervous tick can be addressed by suggesting that the candidate relocate the impulse to another, less visible part of the body, such as squeezing toes inside shoes. Feedback about length and focus of responses given may take more time and investment from the advisor and faculty panelists to effect positive change in the interviewee. Too much false encouragement may also (mis)shape the candidates' ongoing preparation. And of course, all these mock interview steps generally must be accomplished in a short window of time—all while advisors balance other job responsibilities and students manage full schedules.

As with most aspects of the mock interview process, adjustments must be made for the unique academic and service interests of the candidate, even while recognizing such individualism may not emerge fully in the actual interview space itself—and certainly will not shape the proceedings. The most seemingly polished candidate is likely to feel apprehensive when faced with a high-stakes interview situation; sharing strategies for controlling nerves should be standard in preparing candidates, as should many of the strategies and practical advice outlined previously in this essay. Given the variety of campuses and candidates NAFA members serve, and judging from the authors' survey data and qualitative comments, the following best practices are suggested when arranging in-person mock interviews for major awards.

Advisors should obtain suitable space on campus for the mock interview. Squeezing everyone into an advisor's office will not approximate the actual experience best, so appropriate rooms need to be reserved. There needs to be space for the panel and interviewee to sit comfortably in a location that approximates an actual award interview space. Advisors should also consider the type of questions asked in the respective interviews, preparing a list of the type of questions the student may receive at the actual interview and tailoring the questions toward the specific candidate. (This list of questions may be useful for the candidate to review after conducting the mock interview itself, as another stage of the preparation.)

The authors' survey data underscore that it is vital to engage faculty in mock interviews. Inviting faculty known to be student friendly will provide the best mock interview experience. Including faculty unfamiliar to the student will also model the experience itself more closely, although that is not always possible on smaller campuses. Inviting at least one additional faculty member outside the student's discipline is likely to mimic the diverse makeup of the actual panel, and doing so will also have the advantage of garnering more varied feedback. (Inviting deans and other upper administrators can also bring a wealth of experience to the mock interview situation and at the same time enlighten such campus community members about the office's efforts and procedures on and beyond campus.) When inviting participation on mock interview panels, advisors should be mindful of schedules and other practicalities. It is best to start with the candidate's availability and build around that timetable, ensuring that the interviewers, who are likely to have full calendars, have time options. It is also important to allow for the negative answer. Advisors planning more than one mock interview should be careful to invite discipline-specific faculty to the appropriate availability slots. Asking for as much flexibility as possible and providing deadlines for responses will achieve the completion of a desired schedule in a timely manner.

As soon as the appointed mock interview time is set, advisors should be sure to let the candidate know, sharing the names of those on the panel and the timeline. The candidate's application materials should then be shared with those agreeing to participate in the mock interview (asking them to keep them in confidence, of course) and panelists should be asked to familiarize themselves with those materials appropriately. Advisors also regularly provide sample questions (garnered from previous candidates' experiences or from what the major awards' leaders share about their expected processes and practices) to mock interview panelists. It is also important to provide a description of the award or a link to the award's website so panelists know at least the broad strokes of the opportunity for which the candidate is being considered.

At the mock interview, the advisor will likely want to bring the panel together before the start of the interview. Scheduling their arrival for thirty minutes before that of the candidate ensures the advisor can have the room set up, review any questions interviewers may have, and outline the order of questions to be asked. It can be helpful for the advisor to lay out some rules for the procedure too—designating one interviewer for the "tough" questions, for example, or requesting that a particular scenario be handled by a specific panelist. Practice interviews are generally intended to be as realistic an experience as possible; sharing this with panelists as well as the structure in place for the under-thirty-minute encounter will make for a better experience for all participants. The advisor may need to remind panelists that the *candidate* should spend the most time talking. Additionally, the advisor may need to guide panelists as to approach and then run the interview as close to the real experience as possible, including having the candidate dress appropriately, be timely, and wait outside the room to be invited in at the appropriate moment.

On many campuses, the advisor may have to be an active participant in these procedures but, if possible, they should remain neutral as an observer. In that role, then, the advisor can monitor and provide further feedback after the experience. Advisors should enable the panel to give direct feedback to the applicant too, being careful to step in and moderate as needed should the panel's responses veer counter to advisors' own expertise in this area. After excusing the candidate, advisors can gather any further feedback from panelists more directly and thank the panel for their participation and input. If faculty and upper administrators give their time to support advisors' efforts, make sure to thank them formally (copying faculty members' department chairs on the thank-you email or snail mail letter can be helpful for faculty members); doing so promptly may nudge their agreement toward serving again in the future. It is important to let all volunteers know ultimate outcomes as well. After practice interviews have been completed, advisors can debrief with candidates individually. Doing so will allow advisors to manage any disappointment the candidate may have felt about their performance, as well as address any unhelpful feedback that may have been shared. Advisors can also then offer suggestions about the candidate's ongoing preparations, though overpreparation is also to be avoided.[8] Rehearsed or canned answers should be discouraged, since interview committees are eager to meet authentic students.

The virtual realm, of course, offers many of the same opportunities as the in-person experience, but it can bring some distinct challenges. Again, approximating the actual experience as closely as possible is important, and many of the aspects for in-person coordination extend to the virtual environment. Additional factors to consider for virtual mock interviews specifically include carefully setting up and ensuring functioning technology for the virtual space, as well as preparing candidates to advocate for themselves if they are having difficulty hearing any of the interviewers. Students should also be encouraged not to mute and unmute themselves, as the awkwardness that arises between using and forgetting the button can inhibit the flow of the interview. Both candidates and panelists need to be confident that the meeting has ended before reacting to the content of it. If planning to record the interview for the purpose of review, ensure panelists and candidates are comfortable with this ahead of time. Provide the candidate with access to the recording after the mock interview and debriefs have been conducted. It may be helpful for the candidate to watch the mock interview with the advisor, as the advisor can help guide reflection and interpretation accordingly. Similarly, advisors may want to watch interview insights shared by the foundations, such as the those shared by Rhodes.[9]

Conclusions

From the overview of campus best practices, the survey, and exchanges with major award personnel, the authors determined that interview advising practices vary across campuses, as might be expected. Even given the variance across NAFA campuses and student bodies, survey data reveal commonalities that direct advisors toward the best practices outlined in this essay. It is nearly universal that advisors offer one-on-one advising to interviewees and provide at least one or two mock interviews that are intentionally designed to be challenging. Individual interview experiences vary, but through such undertakings advisors can play an important role in preparing candidates to engage fully and successfully in a stressful environment. Being equipped to best support finalists should they reach the exciting stage of being a finalist is an important role for fellowships advisors.

Advisors can be helpful to each other and to their candidates by collaborating. Many NAFA members have shared their experiences through the survey, in the organization's Slack channels, and at regional and national gatherings to ensure that no advisor is an island in such interview preparations. While some campuses may have experience in preparing candidates in several successive years, other institutions may have little to no (or infrequent) engagement with these major awards' processes and procedures, as the survey data about average number of candidates selected for interviews reveal. Advisors sharing their students' experiences with the NAFA community could be very helpful to an advisor navigating these waters for the first time. Additionally, sharing ideas about how to engage the campus community, such as inviting deans and discipline-specific faculty to partner on such efforts, can only support other NAFA members in building and furthering campus connections to the award advising office. And other prospective candidates may become more aware of possibilities because campus faculty are expanding their awareness and outreach in their classes and departments as well. The major awards have recently indicated their awareness of the stress and significance of the interview as the last step toward awards: on their respective websites, Rhodes includes snapshots of the experience from recent awardees, and Marshall provides advice about its interviews (including several videos that can be watched on YouTube, as well as a PDF).

The significance of the interview is clear—it is the last border to cross into the status of awardee. While every interview experience will be as varied as the candidate selected for the opportunity, preparing candidates to understand expectations and to feel more relaxed in the interview environment is fundamental work for major award advisors. This essay suggests key interview elements to share with candidates. A survey of best practices across NAFA members reveals that advisors are dedicated to using campus resources and expertise to support students, maximizing their talents and successes.

Appendix: NAFA Survey on Mock Interview Practices

Survey question	Response options
Average number of finalists who have interviews annually (all fellowships)	0, 1–4, 5–10, 11–20, >20
Resources used to prepare finalists	Mock interview, one-on-one advising, workshops, peer advising, written resources (articles, books, websites, etc.), other
If you offer finalists a mock interview, how many do you offer (on average)?	1, 2, 3, 4 or more
Who helps you with the mock interviews?	Fellowships advisors, faculty, deans, staff, former finalists/scholars, graduate students, other finalists in the same year, other
If your committee takes an intentional stance in the mock interview, how do they do that?	Role playing with tough questions
	Asking a committee member to be disruptive or even hostile
	Having each committee member ask the same number of questions, or the opposite
	Bringing in a disciplinary expert to test the candidate's in-field knowledge
	Having a committee member ask an uninformed question

Appendix (continued)

Survey question	Response options
	Having a committee member ask a confusing/not well articulated question
	Having a committee member ask if the student would be willing to change their proposal
	Manufacturing distractions (loud noises, yawning, running late, etc.)
Does your campus share questions and/or reports gathered from previous candidates' interview experiences?	Yes/no
Do you record mock interviews and provide them to candidates for their own review?	Yes/no
If yes, do you allow other candidates to review these videos?	Yes/no
What kind of follow-up do you have with finalists post-interview?	One-on-one debrief, interview report, workshop/panel, group advising, other

Notes

1. This essay grew from a 2021 NAFA conference virtual presentation, including the data supporting this discussion.
2. The survey questions and possible responses are included as an appendix to this essay.
3. "Application Overview: The Interview," Rhodes Trust, https://www.rhodeshouse.ox.ac.uk/scholarships/application-overview/; "Interviews," Marshall Scholarships, https://www.marshallscholarship.org/apply/interviews.
4. "The Mitchell Scholarship," US-Ireland Alliance, https://www.us-irelandalliance.org/mitchellscholarship/applicants. Editors' note: Just as this volume of essays was going to press, Trina Vargo, president of the US-Ireland Alliance, announced that there would be a pause in awarding the Mitchell Scholarship for Fall 2025.
5. The authors exchanged emails with representatives of each of the four major awards explored here; the same questions were posed to each representative, and their responses inform this discussion.

6. Students should be cautioned against allowing note-taking to disrupt the flow of conversations in interviews. See Tara Yglesias, "Enough about Me, What Do You Think about Me? Surviving the Truman Interview," in *Wild about Harry: Everything You Have Ever Wanted to Know about the Truman Scholarship*, ed. Suzanne McCray and Tara Yglesias (Fayetteville: University of Arkansas Press, 2021), 91–103.

7. "Practice Interview Questions," Harry S. Truman Scholarship Foundation, https://www.truman.gov/apply/finalists/practice-interview-questions/.

8. See Tara Yglesias, "Suspenders and a Belt: Overpreparation and the Overachiever," in McCray and Yglesias, *Wild about Harry*, 43–51.

9. See Rhodes Trust, "Interview Tips: Applying for the Rhodes Scholarship," YouTube video, 18:25, posted October 6, 2023, https://www.youtube.com/watch?v=T556Z-txmbE.

3

What Did I Do Wrong?

Counseling the Unsuccessful Fellowship Applicant

GREGORY A. LLACER

The reality of a fellowships advisor's work is that condolences are offered more often than congratulations. The expectations of applicants, particularly neophytes, are often so high that the first question asked after a rejection is typically, *What did I do wrong?* The purpose of this essay is to examine this question and its genesis, and to explore strategies for redirecting the emotional energy that accompanies a rejection into a conversation that is meaningful, useful, supportive, and forward thinking.

In general, as a counselor (not critic!), it is essential to provide support to the applicant throughout the process, which includes the postscript. Effective advising practices will help the applicant develop a positive mindset and be encouraged to persevere past the short-term disappointment, which is a much better strategy than attempting to soothe disappointed applicants by telling them that they were clearly a shoo-in, and the fact they were not selected is difficult to believe. Of course, providing resources and tools that can help applicants "improve" their application, such as books, workshops, or online courses, can be helpful but may be a dodge of what otherwise could be a painful but necessary conversation. It is crucial to remind the applicant that rejection is not a reflection of worth and that they should not give up on their goals. It is also critical to point out, preferably at the beginning of the process but also at the end, that the experience of writing a postgraduate fellowship application is also about the exercise of self-reflection, about composition, about communication, and about how to make what essentially is a two-dimensional narrative something that is compelling to read—something that makes the reader want to meet the writer.

Fellowships advisors tend to provide significantly more guidance about broad strategies at the beginning of the process than at the end. However, steering the deceptively simple *What did I do wrong?* question to a forward-looking goal can be an instructive tool and provide a greater awareness of variables to consider in future applications, not only for fellowships but for graduate school applications, professional employment searches, and other endeavors for which there is a competitive written process.

To be fair, most fellowships advisors do this routinely with applicants, but the tendency for applicants, especially first-timers, is to get lost in the process and consumed with the outcome and to forget many of the philosophical and practical considerations as they put together their materials. After the fact, these reminders may need to be addressed in a different way, but the possibility for a recollection and recognition of potential causal factors looms larger and with a greater understanding of context, especially for those individuals genuinely interested in taking another leap.

Considering a Cursory Review of Literature

Before conducting a review of potentially relevant literature, it is helpful to consider the full range of topics that encompass the rejection of a fellowship applicant. Psychological elements predominate: the feeling of failure, an explicit confirmation of imposter syndrome, fears about what it portends for future opportunities more broadly than the focus of the application itself. Intellectual elements also come into play: an emerging doubt about grounding in a student's area of expertise, a harsh indictment of an applicant's ability to write, a curiosity and maybe an emerging cynicism about whether the student's advocates are truly advocating. And yet, while there is a robust literature on subjects like imposter syndrome in general or rejection in a broader sense (e.g., medical school or graduate school rejection, college application rejection, even job application rejection), very little, if any, data have been collected formally on the attitudes and experiences of postgraduate fellowship applicants, with the notable exception of medical school residencies (which, in all fairness, are a very different type of scholarship).

Still, there are kernels of interesting observations in a few repositories of existing data, in particular on imposter syndrome characteristics that can be applied readily to fellowship applicants. An elegant example, for instance, may be found in the Impostor Cycle, based on the pathbreaking work of Pauline Rose Clance in 1985.[1] The article underscores a need to be aware of the perspectives and experiences of BIPOC (Black, Indigenous, and other people of color) students, first-generation scholars, and students from underserved backgrounds, a significant and topical matter that critically deserves its own treatment beyond the scope of this essay. As a general primer, however, while intended specifically to be applied to BIPOC experiences, the flowchart figure embedded in the article also may be helpful in evaluating what is happening when imposter syndrome is in play with unsuccessful fellowship application outcomes. More importantly, the figure provides a way to consider not only the possibility of imposter syndrome in unsuccessful applicants but also how to approach the other psychological and intellectual hurdles that follow an unexpected (or expected?) negative result of a fellowship application.

Breaking Down the Question

The profile of a typical postgraduate fellowship applicant is someone who has achieved a fair degree of success academically and probably has demonstrated other attributes effectively, such as leadership, service, or a specific scholarly or research pursuit. For many of these types of applications, whether the process has an endorsement component, includes an interview, or is based on an evaluation of the written materials alone, applicants are encouraged to seek guidance. This guidance comes from not only the counselor whose job it is to offer support in the process but also advanced scholars (faculty, but also others with content or writing expertise), employers, and others who ultimately may become advocates through recommendation letters. However, the end game for the unsuccessful applicant, especially given all the advice and encouragement an advisor can muster, can seem more of a binary equation even though so many other variables may be in play.

So when an applicant asks, *What did I do wrong?* it suggests that there must be an exact deficiency that can be defined and corrected "for next time." Indeed, the reflexive question is a natural reaction, and arguably an if-then prospect. If the applicant did not receive the fellowship or endorsement, then there must be something very specific that was identified as a vulnerability in the evaluation of the candidacy. The problem with this kind of thinking is that not only are there a host of implicit variables in the process, but each fellowship is a distinct exercise, similar to yet ultimately different from those that otherwise may seem analogous in type or practice. When first sitting with an unsuccessful candidate, instead of staring at an application and attempting to identify vulnerabilities in the composition, it may be worthwhile simply to talk through the variables first and consider what may have played into the decision-making (especially when the external review process itself is inscrutable). However, a note of caution here: these examples are *possible* variables, not definitive ones. The drawback of sharing this information unvarnished or without nuance is that it may give the unintentional impression that there is an embedded unfairness in the process, which is not the point here. The point is there are so many factors in play in these exercises that to try to isolate a specific independent reason accurately is not only unproductive but also virtually impossible. Some of these recognizable variables include the following:

- *A large, talented candidate pool:* Fellowships, by their design, especially the prestigious awards that undergraduate seniors and early-stage graduate students gravitate toward, attract a rich, robust, and intellectually deep applicant profile. Concerted efforts to diversify classes of fellows beyond traditional, elite applicant bases are starting to bear fruit, and many fellowships advisors now are committed to identifying talent

beyond those individuals who actively seek such awards.
In addition, a growing number of higher education institutions are engaging professional advisors to boost the awareness of awards and programs to individuals who might
otherwise think that such opportunities are not for them. The
result, especially now that travel and international scholarship
are back in force following the pandemic, is that there simply
are too many great candidates for too few opportunities (as
historically has been the case). As applicants dive into self-
reflection and dossier composition, there is a tendency to
turn inward and forget exactly how competitive these opportunities are. Doing so is not necessarily counterproductive—
in fact, to be fully immersed in the practice of writing is
essential—but there does seem to be a tendency to lose sight
of the fact that, for most of these awards, the rote percentage
of selected fellows is extremely small compared with the total
number of applicants.

- *Relative experience of the advisor:* The content knowledge and
  experience of the advisor or mentor play a crucial role in
  the fellowship application evaluation and selection process.
  Advisors who have a strong track record of guiding successful candidates can augment and enhance the work of
  institutional endorsement or selection committees. In particular, their understanding of external program characteristics
  and how awardees are actually selected can carry significant
  weight in evaluating an applicant's potential. If an applicant
  does not seek guidance from someone institutionally who is
  knowledgeable about the process, or only receives perfunctory suggestions, they may not realize their full potential as a
  candidate.

- *Relative experience of endorsement or selection committee
  members:* There may be variations in the subprocess of how
  committee members are chosen, within both educational
  institutions (for endorsement processes) and fellowship
  organizations (for selection processes). An academic institution, for instance, depending on whether faculty receive

service credit for participating in a review committee, may get a specific subset of respondents. In some institutions, such committees are standardized; in others, fellowships advisors must rely on the "good citizens" who step up to participate. Fellowship organizations similarly seek out potential reviewers in a variety of ways and in a variety of combinations that may include individuals who are previous recipients, active government officials, and others whose expertise is compelling to those enterprises. In any case, while diversity and variability can enhance the selection process, they also may lead to unpredictability in the evaluation of applicants, depending on the relative depth of selectors' academic or professional expertise. However, striving for demographic breadth and depth in committee composition can help to ensure that all candidates are fairly evaluated.

- *Unbalanced demographic variables among institutional applicants:* There are two primary ways demographic variables can play into a selection process, particularly within an academic institution's endorsement process. First, a very high number of applicants in a particular disciplinary field may affect a candidate's ability to stand out unless there has been a concerted effort to compose a memorable dossier. Second, a similar qualification applies to a fellowship requiring an applicant to choose a state or region in which their application will be evaluated—too many applicants hailing from one institution may have an unforeseeable and unpredictable impact in a national screening and selection. Yet institutions are right not to discriminate on the basis of such demographic variables; letting the evaluation play out as purely and organically as possible is critical, so that each application is assessed essentially on its merits and strength of connection to the opportunity.

- *A very high bar for applicants to be endorsed or selected:* By definition, postgraduate fellowships are inherently (and sometimes outrageously) competitive, and in general they cater to applicants who can demonstrate brilliant academic achievement, intellectual development through research experience, evidence of formative leadership experience, and a compelling vision for future endeavors. Admirably, fellowship organizations are trending toward seeking talent and promise wherever it may be found, even beyond archetypal institutional profiles. Still, candidates who possess potential or whose story or trajectory is more unconventional may also be at a disadvantage if they fall short of what are usually rigorous and inflexible criteria. In addition, while the criteria may specify an objective way for selectors to compare applicants and render decisions, unique qualities, potential, and personal circumstances may be overlooked, thus discounting individuals who may possess exceptional qualities that ultimately could enhance and diversify the selected cohort.

- *Incorporating a "buckshot" strategy or relying on a single narrative for multiple applications:* The ambitions of some applicants know no bounds. Conversely, some applicants are fairly unclear in their own minds about how they want to approach the future and what they want to accomplish. Both cases may result in the submission of a flurry of postgraduate fellowship applications implementing a corner-cutting strategy by duplicating narrative statements and other components at the expense of truly highlighting an applicant's unique experiences, skills, and aspirations specific to the opportunity. Applicants should approach multiple submissions with caution and be sure to articulate an alignment with the fellowship's goals across all parts of the dossier.

All that having been said, an unsuccessful applicant likely will still desire to discuss the writing process itself and ways to think about composition going forward. Doing so can be a helpful exercise as long as the intent is not so much pinpointing the vulnerabilities in a previous application, which may or may not be actually causative. Instead, it may be worthwhile to reprise the self-reflection exercises that typically begin the application process in order to point out the broader factors that may be less apparent to the applicant, even if such ground was covered at the beginning or at different points in the development of the application.

As an exercise, consider the following four questions and ask applicants to reread and self-evaluate the degree to which they believe they were on the mark relative to the opportunity for which they applied.

How Customized Was the Dossier to the Opportunity?

As indicated earlier, applicants should be mindful about customizing an application with resolve and purpose. Applicants often focus on eligibility requirements as the benchmark for determining whether the fellowship is germane to their interests and goals, as opposed to the description of the fellowship itself. Yet by concentrating on the fellowship description, and looking for both the explicit and more subtle messages conveyed, the applicant will be able to get a clearer perspective on intent and potential fit. Then, in the construction of personal essays, the response to question prompts, and other supplementary pieces of the dossier, applicants can be more fulsome in their narratives and show a deep understanding of the program's aims. In this way, the dossier will seem both tailored and intentional. The applicant has an ability to emphasize their academic foundation, their commitment through dimensional preparation, and most importantly a thorough understanding of the fellowship's mission.

When applying to multiple, related fellowships, applicants may be tempted to copy language from one application and use it in the next. Unfortunately, the lesson often learned too late is that customization and attention to detail are essential for success in fellowship applications. A desire for efficiency is understandable, as applicants are balancing their school and personal responsibilities at a very busy time in their lives. In some cases, applicants are balancing so many responsibilities that the editing process gets shortchanged, resulting in unintended references to other programs, which can be the death knell for someone who otherwise may be a contender.

(By the way, this also happens to even the most attentive recommender, who likely has many, many letters to compose. If fellowships advisors can get ahead of this particular problem with faculty before the final submission, it is an effort well spent.)

How Responsive Was the Author to the Prompts in the Application?

Beyond looking at the broader task of customizing the dossier, a more granular approach should be applied to the essay prompts in the application. Of special consideration is the degree to which a prompt examines more than one point. This could be evident in multiple questions within the same prompt, or a question with more than one element that needs to be addressed. When an applicant feels more comfortable with one aspect of the prompt or question, there will be more emphasis placed on that focus, which inherently compromises a generous response to the other part of the question—especially when there is a word or character limit.

The other challenge, of course, is that the applicant may have a lot to say but not a lot of space to say it (again, because of the limit). Thus, the Goldilocks principle applies—not too much, not too little, but just right. In some unsuccessful applications, it is clear that the balance is off in the narrative because the writer committed to a perspective or narrative that requires extensive explanation but may not actually address the prompt.

Did the author effectively communicate their ideas without unnecessary jargon or ambiguity? Were their responses to the prompts succinct, while still providing sufficient information? Digging deep requires the applicant to fully immerse themselves in the narrative and apply an efficient and measured approach that does two things simultaneously: gets to the essence of the question, however complex, with thoroughness and substance, and provides enough detail to satisfy themselves that the response reflects their intellectual and personal identity honestly and forthrightly.

How Cohesive Were All the Elements in the Dossier?

Essentially, all fellowship applications share similar components, such as essays, transcripts, and letters of recommendation. In some cases, applicants are asked to respond to very specific questions. Perhaps a curriculum vitae is a required component. However the dossier is constructed, a high degree of cohesion should exist that connects every element in an effective, logical way. The unity of a dossier is a useful quality to consider, particularly because many unsuccessful applicants are likely to consider each element in isolation. In doing so, they often are providing excellent, essential information, but the question of cohesion may have escaped them. In thinking about how all the elements of a dossier hold together, both with respect to logic and in consideration of breadth and depth relative to the opportunity, unsuccessful applicants can determine what may not have been fully connected and thereby be better prepared for future applications.

And so strategic communication and design are integral to achieving cohesion in a fellowship application dossier. Clear and concise writing, attention to detail, and thoughtful organization contribute to the overall cohesiveness of the elements. A well-structured dossier with consistent formatting, grammar, and style fosters the ability to make a positive impression and ensures that the flow of information within a dossier is choreographed in a readable, linear fashion without tangents or jumpiness. Moreover, the use of a consistent tone and language across all elements helps create a coherent and unified narrative.

Practically speaking, getting feedback on drafts is fundamental, and many unsuccessful applicants simply do not get enough information that could be helpful in crafting revisions. However, before doing so, the applicant should thoroughly analyze and edit each element of the dossier to ensure consistency in syntax, grammar, tone, and formatting. Then, the applicant should share narratives with trusted advocates—not only with their recommenders but also with others who may be instructive in refining the narrative to strengthen the overall cohesion of the dossier.

Most importantly, the key to cohesion in a dossier is how all the pieces fit together. Like the adage goes, "The whole is greater than the sum of its parts." Some application processes (for instance the application for the Truman Scholarship) have many, if not all, the components indicated earlier and also require responses to a number of seemingly disparate questions. How do all the components fit together comprehensively? Does the policy statement connect to the public service experience? If not, what are the connecting intellectual threads that bind all the responses, previous experience, goals for the fellowship, and aspirations for the future? Virtually all the well-known postgraduate fellowships have similar appraising variables. For instance, the Rhodes Scholarship assesses the following: academic success, evidence of service, an extramural passion, and leadership, *plus* an intent to engage in one or more programs of study, specifically at Oxford. How do those elements, individually and collectively, coalesce into a memorable, compelling whole that defines the candidate without leaving out or rendering relatively weak any one of them?

How Empathetic Was the Writing?

Finally, what does it mean to be an "empathetic" writer? In communicating one's own idea to someone else, it is especially important for a young author to consider how what they articulate is consumed and digested by someone who does not know them, their aspirations, or their motivations. To be able to take themselves out of the composition and attempt to assess it from another perspective sometimes is a challenge that elevates the construction of the narrative to a more complicated level. Yet doing so can draw a greater, more effusive connection, not only to those who read the dossier but to the candidate as well. Such introspection serves to create a dimensional understanding of purpose and the applicant's own motivations, which in turn is reflected in the selectors' evaluation.

Empathy tends to be an undervalued characteristic among young scholars, especially if they approach exercises such as writing applications (whether they be for fellowships, graduate school, or something else) with an exigent need to make sure the reader knows who they are on their own terms. Generally speaking, empathy doesn't come up as an elemental strategy very often and frequently takes a back seat to establishing identity, which is also a significant undertaking, to form the applicant's connection to the fellowship and all its intents. Nevertheless, the review of an unsuccessful application by an author who is open to trying to take the view on the other side of the table has the potential to be very instructive as other opportunities appear.

Conclusion

Identifying specific causal factors that contribute to the rejection of a fellowship application is a dicey prospect, and in counseling individuals who are not successful it is important to assure them that there could be a variety of reasons that they were not chosen. Variables such as the volume of applications, the likely talent within the pool, demographic breadth, and high selection standards could singularly or collectively influence an outcome. Fellowships advisors can be influential at the end of the process, in helping candidates understand these variables after the fact, so that they are less inclined to blame themselves or think that there may have been elements in the process that unfairly excluded them from thoughtful consideration.

It is key to reorient the conversation from looking back to looking forward, reflecting on how the applicant could further consider four specific elements that contribute to a memorable dossier: how to customize the content to fit the opportunity, how to be fully responsive to prompts, how to shape an application that is cohesive (this includes how the opportunity aligns with prior experiences and goals for the future). Such self-reflection and connection of the intellectual, social, and personal threads can strengthen the reason and logic of the candidacy and increase the potential for success.

At all stages in the process, a fellowship advisor can be a source of support and offer constructive guidance, especially after an unsuccessful application attempt. To counter the possibly weighty emotional impact, it is important to note that there is no correlation between rejection and potential. Redirecting the emotional reaction into a meaningful conversation about how best to move forward after the fact can help an applicant gain greater insights about navigating an application, reiterating that putting their hat in the ring is first and foremost an exercise in self-reflection, composition, and empathic communication. By engaging in thorough, meaningful conversations and encouraging self-reflection, advisors contribute to the overall resilience and success of applicants in their pursuit of postgraduate fellowships, graduate school, and other competitive opportunities.

Notes

1. Afran Ahmed et al., "Why Is There a Higher Rate of Imposter Syndrome among BIPOC?," *Across the Spectrum of Socioeconomics* 1, no. 2 (2020): 1–17; Jaruwan Sakulku and James Alexander, "The Impostor Phenomenon," *International Journal of Behavioral Science* 6, no. 1 (2011): 73–92; Pauline R. Clance, *The Impostor Phenomenon: Overcoming the Fear That Haunts Your Success* (Atlanta: Peachtree, 1985).

PART II

Increasing Access

4

Community College and Transfer Student Access to Nationally Competitive Awards

CASSIDY ALVARADO

Growing up in New Berlin, Wisconsin, a small suburb of Milwaukee, I was expected to attend a four-year university because of my good grades and cocurricular activities. My brother, however, had less than stellar grades and struggled in high school. His plan was to graduate as soon as possible and attend a two-year technical school in order to earn money quickly. As I took out significant student loans to pay for a yet unknown career, he immediately began earning a steady paycheck as a machinist apprentice, working in a trade that challenged and fulfilled him.

At the time, I considered my brother's pathway to be the lesser one, and while I received praise and admiration for getting into a state university, his decision was treated with apathy. In my high school, community college was never discussed as an option for above-average or even average students. Instead, we were told that two-year schools were either for remedial students or to learn a trade. As a first-generation college student, I was ignorant of the benefits of attending a community college, such as its affordability and the opportunity it provided to explore courses and careers before committing to a major or degree program.

Unsurprisingly, as a new fellowships advisor in 2013, I was initially skeptical when a transfer student from a two-year school told me that she was interested in applying for a Marshall Scholarship. A post-traditional student,[1] she had had a circuitous journey through higher education and had most recently attended a community college before transferring to the state school where I worked.

After our first advising session, however, I knew I had a lot to learn about community college and transfer students. That student became my first Marshall candidate. She not only excelled academically but also had extensive professional experience, maturity, and strong motivation, all of which earned her a finalist interview. Although she was not ultimately selected, supporting her through the application process inspired me to examine my own implicit bias against community college students. Years later, when I began my doctoral studies, I committed to researching community college and transfer student access to nationally competitive awards (NCAs). My goal was to better understand this frequently overlooked population and inform practices that would encourage and support their fellowship applications.

First, I conducted a comprehensive literature review to learn about community college transfer student success and stigma. I discovered that approximately six million students attend two-year institutions.[2] This population is ethnically and racially diverse: 56 percent of Hispanic undergraduate students and 44 percent of Black undergraduate students attend two-year institutions, and most of these students also hail from the lowest socioeconomic groups.[3] Moreover, around 42 percent of first-generation college students attended two-year institutions, compared with 26 percent of students whose parents had earned a bachelor's degree.[4]

I also learned that around 33 percent of community college students transfer to a four-year institution,[5] and although transfer students from community colleges represent a significant population in higher education, they experience barriers and challenges that affect their success, such as being underestimated after transferring to their four-year institutions. These challenges also include the false perception among faculty that they "are not academically prepared for the rigor of the course work in the university environment."[6]

After learning more about this population, I continued reviewing the literature on NCAs, specifically surrounding access and benefits. Also known as prestigious scholarships and fellowships, these awards are generally considered the "gold standard for students who will become future leaders and benefit from a lifetime of advantages that the award offers."[7]

Existing literature on NCAs is limited and generally focuses on the experiences of alumni (typically initiated by the funding organization) or includes firsthand accounts of advisors and faculty who support students in the application process. While both approaches to the field are inherently problematic because neither addresses possible issues with the selection processes, they do illustrate the benefits of NCAs beyond a monetary value. For example, a Fulbright alumni survey showed that participants felt their NCA experience helped them clarify their professional goals.[8] Additionally, Lia Rushton, a fellowships advisor since the early 1990s, argues that students who apply for NCAs learn how to articulate their academic and career goals through the process of self-reflection, sometimes earlier in their undergraduate careers than those who do not apply for these types of opportunities.[9]

Although studies connected to NCA access are limited, literature does reveal that some foundation directors have expressed concern over "missing many qualified individuals, often from groups under-represented" in their application pools.[10] Moreover, Terri Heath and colleagues note that otherwise-qualified students may fail to obtain an NCA "because the student lacks information about the availability of these resources or because the student lacks knowledge about how to compete successfully for limited funds."[11] It is clear that community college and transfer students are a diverse yet desirable population for scholarship opportunities, but what has not been understood is what, if anything, prevents them from applying.

Recognizing a gap in the literature, I then designed a mixed-methods exploratory study to ascertain what prospective and current transfer students from community colleges knew about NCAs and to identify factors that influence their motivation to apply. I also sought to address the question of who is missing from these applicant pools and why. To do so, I focused on the following exemplars: the Benjamin A. Gilman International Scholarship Program, the Fulbright US Student Program, the Jack Kent Cooke

Undergraduate Transfer Scholarship, and the Harry S. Truman Scholarship. These awards were selected because of their exceptional benefits and suitability for both the community college and transfer student populations. Each award also has a time-intensive and time-sensitive application and most require campus support, usually in the form of an institutional endorsement or nomination process. Two descriptive research questions guided my study: What do transfer students from community colleges know about NCAs, and what primary factors influence their decision to apply?

I utilized Samuel Museus's Culturally Engaging Campus Environments (CECE) model as the theoretical framework for my study because of its focus on how higher education institutions can support the success of diverse student populations like students from community colleges.[12] The CECE model is based on research that shows the more a campus is culturally engaging, especially regarding diverse student populations, the more likely students are to succeed on that campus. As illustrated in Figure 4.1, the model shows that

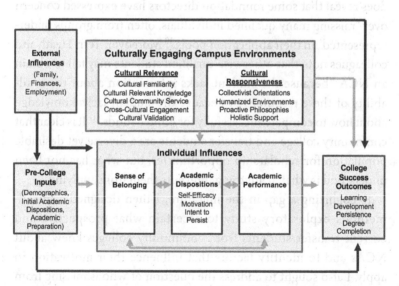

Figure 4.1. Used with permission from Samuel Museus, "The Culturally Engaging Campus Environments (CECE) Model: A New Theory of Success among Racially Diverse College Student Populations," in *Higher Education: Handbook of Theory and Research*, ed. M. B. Paulsen, HATR, vol. 29 (New York: Springer, 2014), 207. Copyright © 2014 Springer. Reprinted with permission.

student success is directly tied to external influences, such as family, finances, and employment; precollege inputs, such as demographics and academic preparedness; individual influences, such as self-efficacy, a sense of belonging, and academic performance; and nine culturally engaging campus environment factors.[13]

To measure motivation to apply to NCAs, I focused on external influences, individual influences, and cultural responsiveness campus environment factors, or how campus environments support diverse students. In the CECE model, the four cultural responsiveness campus environment factors are *collectivist cultural orientations*, or to what extent campuses are promoting collaborative group environments versus validating individual efforts; *humanized environments*, or to what extent campuses employ faculty and staff who care about and develop meaningful relationships with their students; *proactive philosophies*, or to what extent campuses employ faculty and staff who make the extra effort of bringing pertinent information and support directly to the students versus just making information and support available to them; and *holistic support*, or to what extent campuses employ faculty and staff who are willing to assist students even when it may be outside their roles and responsibilities. While examining transfer student motivation to apply to NCAs was a new application of the CECE model, the components of the model fit well, given transfer student demographics and common factors that affect college students.

My study used a mixed-methods approach, employing both qualitative and quantitative components. I began with qualitative interviews, followed by the development of a survey, and finished with the distribution of the newly created quantitative survey instrument.[14] Participants in the study included both transfer students from community colleges and currently enrolled community college students who indicated intentions to transfer to a four-year institution. To maintain confidentiality, I used pseudonyms for all participants and their higher education institutions.

Beginning with the qualitative stage, I conducted ten interviews with transfer students from community colleges, including one recent alumnus who had graduated in May 2020. All ten interview participants attended Blue Private University (BPU), a private four-year institution on the West Coast. According to the university website, BPU is a suburban private university with an undergraduate population of around eight thousand. Because of safety concerns during the COVID-19 pandemic, I held these forty-five-minute interviews virtually using Zoom.

To ensure a diverse participant pool, students who expressed interest in participating in the study completed a preinterview form that collected demographic info such as race and ethnicity, major, and Federal Pell Grant status. This form also asked if they had heard of the NCAs in the study and if they had previously applied for any of these awards. Using the form responses, I intentionally interviewed participants from diverse demographic backgrounds and with varying levels of awareness of NCAs. This ensured the study captured multiple transfer student viewpoints.

I designed my interview questions to capture their knowledge of NCAs and factors that potentially influence their decision to apply. I then coded their responses using Dedoose software, looking for emergent themes, especially those that related to the CECE model, such as the importance of self-efficacy in student success, or the belief in their ability to successfully achieve a task. My interview participants with lower self-efficacy were less likely to pursue NCAs. For example, when I asked Athena, a sophomore sociology major with a 3.41 GPA, why she might not apply, she replied, "I kind of psych myself out. And it's like, I know that I can be a great student and I know I can write beautifully. But when I think about it, there's so many other people out there, like, maybe they can write better than me. I mean . . . they can do it better than me. So why am I even trying? I'm not going to get it. So, I psyched myself out like that pretty often. And that would probably be the reason why I wouldn't do it [apply to NCAs]."

By speaking with students who had already transferred to four-year institutions from two-year institutions, I gained insight into obstacles or challenges that limited their access, awareness, and knowledge of NCAs.

For the second part of my study, I invited 3,539 Ocean Community College students to participate in a quantitative survey. The survey asked participants if they were broadly aware of NCAs; if they were aware of the specific NCAs selected for the study, based on eligibility determined by demographic information; and their motivation to apply, which included the CECE campus environment factors.

After comparing self-provided demographic information against the NCA exemplar eligibility, the survey's skip logic presented the appropriate questions for these specific awards. For instance, if respondents indicated they were US citizens who received Federal Pell Grants, they would see questions related to the Gilman Scholarship, beginning with a brief description of the award.

Since there were no existing instruments that measure motivation to apply to NCAs, I also adapted the campus environment questions from Museus and Natasha Saelua's CECE survey for two-year college students.[15] For example, to measure the factor of proactive philosophies, the survey asked respondents to indicate their level of agreement with the following four statements: people at this institution often send me important information about new learning opportunities, people at this institution send me important information about nationally competitive awards, people at this institution often send me important information about supports that are available, and people at this institution check in with me regularly to see if I need support. After creating composite scores for each campus environment factor (collectivist cultural orientations, humanized environments, proactive philosophies, and holistic support), I confirmed a good internal reliability of 0.80 or above, which indicates that the survey questions measured what they intended. I then analyzed the survey data descriptively to better understand the sample demographics, determine knowledge of NCAs among community college students, and gain a general sense of the motivating factors associated with applying.

To answer my first research question (*What do transfer students from community colleges know about NCAs?*), I conducted analyses of the interviews and survey responses and determined that both groups had limited awareness and knowledge of NCAs. For example, although survey respondents were most likely to be eligible for the Fulbright US Student Program (84.8 percent), less than 9 percent had heard of the award. Table 4.1 provides a snapshot of the data collected relating to knowledge and awareness of NCAs.

To answer my second research question (*What primary factors influence transfer students' decision to apply for NCAs?*), I first assessed general interest among the interview participants and survey respondents. All ten interview participants demonstrated interest in at least one of the NCA exemplars, and around 84 percent of survey respondents stated they were strongly or somewhat interested in learning more about NCAs.

Drawing from Museus's CECE model, I then organized factors influencing motivation to apply into three categories: external influences, individual influences, and campus environment characteristics. When I coded interview responses, I discovered that the most frequently referenced external influence was the financial amount of the award. For example, when discussing the Gilman Scholarship, Carlos asserted that he never intended to study abroad due to cost, explaining, "I thought [study abroad] was for people with money, to be honest. I thought I needed a lot of money to do it." Next, looking at individual influences, the most frequently referenced factor was the time and effort to apply. When I asked Henry why he might not apply for an NCA, he answered, "Not any legit reasons but like other than maybe it has too many steps to do . . . like . . . really, really long essays." And finally, when I coded campus environment factors, I discovered that proactive philosophies, which prompted staff and faculty to not only share information with students but also offer support alongside the information, were most frequently referenced. For example, Hannah shared that after she transferred to BPU, she received "bi-weekly or monthly emails . . . with all the fellowship and scholarship information," including emails about several of the exemplars like Truman and Fulbright.

I then analyzed the survey responses. For prospective transfer students from community colleges, the highest-ranked external influence was the financial amount of the award, with around 80 percent

Table 4.1

Integrated Results Matrix of Knowledge and Awareness of NCAs

Qualitative results	Quantitative results	Example quote
The majority of participants had awareness of one or more of the NCA exemplars but could not define what they funded.	The majority of respondents had not heard of the NCA exemplars.	Gema: "I've heard of [Gilman], but I don't know what like the details are of the scholarship."
Knowledge of NCAs was minimal and primarily limited to participants who had applied to one or more of these awards.	Knowledge of NCAs was almost nonexistent, with only four participants correctly providing an example of these awards.	Penelope: "I just applied for some scholarships for graduate school . . . I don't know if those are nationally competitive, though, you know, so . . . I don't know the correct definition."
Participants were most aware of the Fulbright US Student Program.	Respondents were most aware of the Jack Kent Cooke Undergraduate Transfer Scholarship.	Marty: "I know that it's called Fulbright and to my limited understanding based on, I think, the poster that I may have seen . . . it also has something to do with studying abroad or some sort of international program."
Participants were least aware of the Truman Scholarship.	Respondents were least aware of the Gilman Scholarship.	Athena: "I'm glad like, I found out about [Truman] I don't think I've . . . I think I've heard about it, but I don't think I ever actually paid attention to what it was."

Note: I integrated qualitative data (interviews) and quantitative data (survey responses) to provide a side-by-side summary of the data for research question 1.

of respondents selecting it as "extremely important" or "very important" to their motivation to apply. For individual factors, the highest-ranked factor was personal growth, with around 87 percent of respondents selecting it as "extremely important" or "very important" to their motivation to apply. Of the four campus environment factors measured in this study, survey respondents rated humanized educational environments highest. Composite data showed around 54 percent of Ocean Community College respondents felt that their campus cared about them and only 4 percent "disagreed" or "strongly disagreed" with these scale items. Therefore, Ocean Community College was most successful in creating a campus environment where faculty and staff care about their students. Table 4.2 summarizes qualitative and quantitative data on motivation.

My study had several limitations, particularly during the quantitative survey stage. First, due to COVID-19, two of the three confirmed community college sites withdrew their participation in the survey phase, citing new communication policies during the pandemic. Second, although the survey was sent to students enrolled at Ocean Community College, respondents indicated enrollment at twelve unique community college sites. Therefore, my study cannot confirm that prospective transfer student respondents were answering the survey questions based on their experiences at Ocean Community College, rather than their experience at a different community college, or some amalgamation of their entire community college experience. This factor mostly affected the analysis of the CECE scale items, which were designed to measure one campus environment at a time.[16] Additionally, the low response rate of 4.83 percent hinders generalizability. Finally, 75 percent of the survey respondents identified as female; therefore, male and nonbinary perspectives were limited.

Data from both the interviews and the survey overwhelmingly showed that transfer students had minimal awareness of NCA opportunities, including the study exemplars. Regardless of their limited or nonexistent awareness, most participants and respondents were not only eligible for at least one of the study exemplars, but they also showed high levels of interest in learning more about these

Table 4.2
Integrated Results Matrix of Factors that Influence NCA Motivation

Qualitative results	Quantitative results	Example quote
Interest		
All participants demonstrated interest in at least one of the study exemplars.	The majority of respondents were interested in learning more about NCAs.	Saul: "Yeah, I mean, [Gilman] would be something I'd be interested in. Yeah."
External influences		
Participants most frequently referenced "finances," especially as they related to the amount of the NCA.	Respondents ranked "financial amount of the award" as most important.	Henry: "So once again, just to clarify, [Fulbright] pays for, like, your travel there, back, your tuition there and your housing and food? Wow."
Participants least frequently referenced "timing."	Respondents ranked "peer encouragement" as least important.	Carlos: "I looked at the Gilman, but . . . it was too late for me to apply."
Individual influences		
Participants most frequently referenced "self-efficacy."	Respondents ranked "personal growth" as most important.	Alex: "But I think something that did discourage me is if I saw the requirements and I was like, 'oh, I definitely don't cut this.'"
Participants least frequently referenced "sense of belonging."	Respondents ranked "resume builder" as least important.	Vika: "I just wanted to transfer out [of Beach Community College] and [at] BPU I really feel like, oh, I belong, you know?"
Campus factors		
Participants most frequently referenced proactive philosophies.	Respondents found Ocean Community College most successful at creating a humanized educational environment.	Hannah: "I know that like [BPU's fellowships] office will review essays. I also know that [they] can put me in touch with like a mentor that will help me through the [Fulbright] process."
Participants least frequently referenced collectivist cultural orientations.	Respondents found Ocean Community College least successful at demonstrating proactive philosophies.	Gema: "I absolutely love the experience [of Achieve, a club for prospective transfer students]. It felt like a family because everybody . . . it's a network of people who want you to succeed."

Note: I integrated qualitative data (interviews) and quantitative data (survey responses) to provide a side-by-side summary of the data for research question 2.

opportunities. Findings also indicated that external influences, individual influences, and campus factors contributed to their motivation to apply.

Minimal awareness is the first barrier to NCA access and is best summarized by Marty, who said the following during his interview: "I have the motivation. . . . I think the first step would be knowing that [NCAs] exist and knowing that they are actually accessible and realistic to someone like me." While several transfer students did learn about NCAs while attending BPU, seven of the ten participants were unaware that BPU had an office dedicated to NCA support before the study. Transfer students from community colleges typically are only enrolled for a few years at their four-year institutions and should be aware of support services for NCAs as early as possible.

As for external factors, "finances," or more specifically the "financial amount of the award," emerged as the top external influence. Interview participants frequently stated that the amount of an award may influence their interest, especially when assessing the amount of time and effort required to apply. Saul, for instance, called it a "cost-benefit analysis" and calculated a rate on return in terms of how many hours put in versus the potential award amount.

Even though "timing" did not surface as a top motivating factor, it was still a significant finding to discover how many interview participants missed NCA opportunities because they learned about the award after application deadlines, or after their eligibility window had passed. For example, interview participants were least aware of the Truman Scholarship. As interviews for this study were held in April, several of the junior and senior interview participants were surprised to learn that they were no longer eligible and expressed that if they had known about the Truman Scholarship, they would have applied. Because transfer students are learning new systems and support services at their four-year institution, they may be unaware of these deadlines. To account for this transfer adjustment period, Abby Miller highlighted the need for institutions to provide collaborative support for transfers, which includes services like reminders about financial aid deadlines.[17] This same approach may be beneficial in increasing awareness of and access to NCAs that have short eligibility windows, like the Truman Scholarship.

However, timing was also an issue for NCAs with fewer limitations regarding when students can apply. When discussing the Gilman Scholarship, multiple interview participants shared that the timing of when to study abroad was problematic. Even though eligible college students can apply to Gilman as early as freshman year, the question of *when* they should study abroad arose. Several of the survey respondents also indicated a lack of interest in Gilman because they had family or work obligations that prevented them from leaving the country for extended periods of time. These observations reinforce the findings of Monija Amani and Mikyong Minsun Kim, which showed that "personal timing" was a contributing factor in a community college student's decision to study abroad.[18] Therefore, for the Gilman Scholarship, timing is not necessarily about the application deadlines, given that Gilman has two application cycles per year. Instead, the timing issue for Gilman is dependent on the study abroad support and guidance for transfer students. It cannot be addressed until two- and four-year institutions develop tailored study abroad strategies and support systems for these populations.

Concerning individual influences, interview participants most referenced self-efficacy; whereas, survey respondents rated personal growth as their top motivating factor. When they referred to their own competitiveness for NCA opportunities, self-efficacy surfaced as a key factor for interview participants. Although most conflated "eligibility" with competitiveness, when the topic was further explored, they explained that they may not be competitive or "good" candidates for an award. Regardless of the terminology used, competitiveness emerged as the top rationale for why they might not apply for an NCA. They also frequently referenced the prestige of NCAs, and with this prestige came misconceptions about eligibility. For example, Alex believed that Fulbright had a high minimum GPA, when in fact the program has no GPA requirements. A few also mentioned "rejection" as a potential demotivator for applying to NCAs. Competitiveness, prestige, and rejection relate strongly to self-efficacy.

While interview participants most frequently referenced self-efficacy as a motivating individual influence, it is pertinent to note that the survey did not include questions that measured the importance of self-efficacy. However, a few text responses hinted at self-efficacy, such as when one respondent wrote "no one ever seems to win" as a rationale for the lack of interest in learning more about NCAs. Thus, self-efficacy may also be an important individual influence for prospective transfer students from community colleges.

My study also looked at campus environments using the CECE factors of collectivist cultural orientations, humanized educational environments, proactive philosophies, and holistic support. Findings indicated that campuses that lacked holistic support were more likely to lack the other three campus environment factors. Similarly, when a campus offered holistic support, other factors were also evident. Thus, if a campus emphasizes a holistic support approach, then the other three factors are likely to follow.

Holistic support first emerged in the study when participants described how they learned or did not learn about NCAs. Two of the ten participants had community college experiences that demonstrated positive examples of holistic support. As a member of Achieve, a club for prospective transfer students, Gema received guidance on the transfer process, and the club also facilitated NCA workshops and brought in guest speakers to share college success strategies. Likewise, Carlos joined a peer mentor program at Mass Community College in which he was paired with an upperclassman who was attending a nearby four-year institution. It was Carlos's peer mentor who first introduced him to NCAs. They also had in-depth conversations about the transfer process and Carlos's future academic and professional goals.

Conversely, of the five interview participants who recalled hearing about NCAs at their community college, two learned about these opportunities from faculty, two learned about them from their peers, and one credited their knowledge to a campus-wide email. Notably missing from this group were academic advisors or counselors. All ten interview participants shared their varying experiences with academic counselors, especially as they related to the transfer process. Yet not one participant learned about NCA opportunities from these staff members, and most had less than positive experiences with advisors at their community colleges. Furthermore, of the thirty-one survey respondents who indicated awareness of the study exemplars, only two said they learned about the opportunities from an academic counselor.

Previous literature on academic advising has advocated for a more holistic approach to guiding and supporting students, such as Edna Martinez and Chinasa Elue's study on the role of community college academic advisors in facilitating conversations about graduate school.[19] Although not all NCAs fund graduate study or postgraduate experiences, it may be beneficial for academic advisors to introduce NCA opportunities during advisement sessions.

Additional benefits of holistic advising connect back to the remaining CECE factors of collectivist cultural orientations, humanized educational environments, and proactive philosophies. When Carlos and Gema shared their experiences of the holistic support structures at their community colleges (e.g., a transfer club and a peer mentoring program), they were also describing the CECE campus factors of collectivist cultural orientations (expressing that they were part of a larger group), proactive philosophies (they were provided not only information but also support), and humanized educational environments (they felt cared for by individuals associated with these programs). NCAs require buy-in from multiple institutional agents on campus to truly facilitate access. Students need to hear about these awards from multiple sources and individuals. Even though BPU had a dedicated fellowships office, most interview participants were unaware of its existence and therefore wanted to learn about NCAs from other, familiar sources on campus, such as faculty. Moreover, participants who did utilize BPU's fellowships office first learned about these awards from staff and faculty at their community college. When four-year institutions, like BPU, have a dedicated fellowships office, they need to introduce its services as early as possible, such as during a transfer orientation. Therefore, while holistic support did not emerge as the top campus factor, it may be the gateway for creating a culturally engaging campus environment. If campuses begin by implementing or increasing holistic support practices, the other factors may follow.

Findings also suggested that two- and four-year institutions can do better in sharing knowledge about NCAs and offering early support. This aligns with existing literature that has recommended that two- and four-year institutions work together to develop support systems.[20] Advisors at four-year institutions should consider participating in transfer orientations to introduce NCA services as early as possible. Partnerships between institution types, such as hosting joint info sessions and workshops, may be another opportunity to encourage and support transfer students.

Considering the limited research on NCAs, future studies should explore the experiences of students who began their undergraduate careers at four-year institutions to determine if similar strategies work with this population as well.

Additionally, since the current study investigated student awareness and knowledge of NCAs, future studies should also assess faculty and staff awareness and knowledge of these opportunities, especially on community college campuses. As stated earlier, holistic support may be the key campus factor that facilitates access to NCAs. Thus, studies from the staff and faculty perspective may result in future promotion of NCAs to their student populations.

Future studies should also further explore the relationship between self-efficacy and motivation to apply for NCAs, which may be a missing recruitment component for both the funding organizations that offer NCAs and higher education institutions that recruit and support applicants. Funding organizations need to clarify who is eligible and competitive, and higher education institutions need to disseminate these criteria in a way that is accessible to the community college and transfer student populations.

As several transfer students mentioned "rejection" or not winning as a possible deterrent to applying to NCAs, future studies should also investigate the potential benefits of applying to these opportunities. Research could identify a group of "nonwinners" to study if students found the process beneficial despite the disappointing outcome.

After synthesizing the findings, I developed the following set of clear and practical recommendations for foundations and higher education institutions. Access to NCAs should be improved at the institutional and funding organization levels. While budget considerations may limit community college training and the expansion of support services, organizations like the National Association of Fellowships Advisors can enlist their members to help community colleges that do not have the financial means to advise students on NCA opportunities.

For foundations and funding organizations, while some awards like Goldwater and Truman[21] have expanded eligibility requirements to include additional nominations of transfer students, more work needs to be done. Expanding the nomination criteria to include this population is insufficient. Funding organizations should consider barriers to their awards, such as when and how students are introduced to these opportunities as well as the timing of application deadlines.

For awards like Gilman and Truman that may be affected by transfer student timing, funding organizations should consider targeted, earlier recruitment for community college students as early as their first year and reiterated throughout their time at their community colleges and transfer institutions. Furthermore, if funding organizations genuinely want to attract these diverse applicants, they should also consider promoting successful community college and transfer students who have previously won these awards. Recently, alumni of the Fulbright US Student Program formed "affinity groups" to highlight and support current Fulbrighters as well as diversify future applicant pools.[22] While the Fulbright US Student Program is not officially associated with these groups, it could encourage alumni to start another affinity group for Fulbrighters who began their studies at a community college or encourage the existing affinity groups to highlight their members who began their studies at a community college.

For higher education institutions, both two- and four-year colleges and universities should adjust their advising practices on campus to reap the advantages of providing holistic support, specifically support that includes conversations about NCAs.

First, campuses could begin by cross-training academic advisors and counselors, as well as faculty and other staff leaders. At a minimum, campus agents should be aware that these opportunities exist and feel comfortable discussing them with students throughout their undergraduate careers. When faculty and staff reinforce NCAs as viable opportunities, it increases the likelihood that students will apply.

Second, at two-year institutions, the role of the transfer advisor is key. Thus, more in-depth training on NCAs may be beneficial. Transfer advisors, in turn, could offer NCA-specific workshops for their students or embed NCA information into existing workshops like those on financial aid or study abroad.

Third, four-year institutions should consider providing NCA information (especially on awards that lessen tuition costs, like the Jack Kent Cooke Undergraduate Transfer Scholarship) in their recruitment materials and, if possible, offer application support such as NCA workshops for prospective transfer students from feeder community colleges to encourage them to apply. This strategy would benefit not only the individual student but also the receiving institution as well.

Fourth, two- and four-year institutions should create or expand programs like Achieve, which already offers scholarship workshops for its members. This type of program embodies all four CECE campus factors and, without a doubt, made a positive impact on Gema's college experience. Programs like Achieve may also increase NCA access.

Nonetheless, the foregoing recommendations primarily focus on individual institution support and approaches; whereas, collaborative programs jointly offered by two- and four-year institutions have also been shown to support transfer students. In addition to Achieve, Gema also participated in a program between Sunny Community College and BPU that brought her to BPU's campus to conduct research during the summer. It was during this program that Gema first learned about Fulbright, which she ultimately applied for. Therefore, existing collaborative partnerships should make a concerted effort to include NCA information as part of their programming.

Transfer students from community colleges are a diverse population. It is precisely their varying lived experiences and tenacity that make them especially compelling candidates for NCAs. As shown in the findings, these students were not only eligible for these opportunities, but they were also highly interested in learning more about them. When fellowships advisors and funding organizations understand community college and transfer student barriers to NCAs, advisors can begin to offer tailored support that is as unique as these students' other academic, professional, and personal needs.

Notes

1. "Post-traditional Students in Higher Education," Postsecondary National Policy Institute, n.d., https://pnpi.org/post-traditional-students/.
2. Scott Ginder, Janice Kelly-Reid, and Farrah Mann, *Enrollment and Employees in Postsecondary Institutions, Fall 2016; and Financial Statistics and Academic Libraries, Fiscal Year 2016* (Washington, DC: US Department of Education, 2017), https://nces.ed.gov/pubs2018/2018002.pdf.
3. Jennifer Ma and Sandy Baum, "Trends in Community Colleges: Enrollment, Prices, Student Debt, and Completion," College Board Research Brief, April 2016, https://research.collegeboard.org/pdf/trends-community-colleges-research-brief.pdf.
4. Emily Forrest Cataldi, Christopher Bennett, and Xianglei Chen, *First-Generation Students College Access, Persistence, and Post-bachelor's Outcomes*, Stats in Brief, Report No. 2018-421 (US Department of Education, 2018), https://nces.ed.gov/pubs2018/2018421.pdf.
5. David Jenkins and John Fink, *Tracking Transfer: New Measures of Institutional and State Effectiveness in Helping Community College Students Attain Bachelor's Degrees* (New York: Community College Research Center, 2016).
6. Carlos Lopez and Stephanie Jones, "Examination of Factors That Predict Academic Adjustment and Success of Community College Transfer Students in STEM at 4-Year Institutions," *Community College Journal of Research and Practice* 41, no. 3 (April 2016): 17.
7. LeAnn Adam, "The Rhodes Scholarship in the Current Era of Student Activism: What Do We Consider 'Prestigious' and Who Benefits?," *Journal of College and Character* 17, no. 3 (August 2016): 198.
8. EurekaFacts, *Evaluation of ECA's English Language Programs: Fulbright English Teaching Assistant Program* (Rockville, MD: EurekaFacts, 2014), https://eca.state.gov/files/bureau/fulbright_eta_june_2014_report.pdf.

9. Lia Rushton, "First, Do No Harm," *Journal of the National Collegiate Honors Council* 18, no. 1 (2017): 7.

10. Alice Stone Ilchman, Warren F. Ilchman, and Mary Hale Tolar, "Strengthening Nationally and Internationally Competitive Scholarships: An Overview," in *The Lucky Few and the Worthy Many: Scholarship Competitions and the World's Future Leaders*, ed. Alice Stone Ilchman, Warren F. Ilchman, and Mary Hale Tolar (Bloomington: Indiana University Press, 2004), 2.

11. D. Terri Heath, Rebecca Adams, and Deborah Lewis Fravel, "Small Research Grants and Academic Fellowships: How Students Can Compete," *Family Relations* 42, no. 4 (1993): 114.

12. Samuel Museus, "The Culturally Engaging Campus Environments (CECE) Model: A New Theory of Success among Racially Diverse College Student Populations," in *Higher Education: Handbook of Theory and Research*, ed. M. B. Paulsen, HATR, vol. 29 (New York: Springer, 2014), 189–227.

13. Museus.

14. John Creswell and Vicki Plano Clark, *Designing and Conducting Mixed Methods Research*, 3rd ed. (New York: Sage, 2017).

15. Samuel Museus and Natasha Saelua, "The Impact of Culturally Engaging Campus Environments on Sense of Belonging," *Review of Higher Education* 40, no. 2 (2017): 187–215.

16. Museus and Saelua.

17. Abby Miller, "Institutional Practices That Facilitate Bachelor's Degree Completion for Transfer Students," *New Directions for Higher Education* 2013, no. 162 (June 2013): 39–50.

18. Monija Amani and Mikyong Minsun Kim, "Study Abroad Participation at Community Colleges: Students' Decision and Influential Factors," *Community College Journal of Research and Practice* 42, no. 10 (August 2017): 678–92.

19. Edna Martinez and Chinasa Elue, "From Community College to Graduate School: Exploring the Role of Academic Advisors in Promoting Graduate Education at Baccalaureate Degree-Granting Community Colleges," *Journal of Higher Education* 9, no. 7 (February 2020): 1003–27.

20. Barbara Tobolowsky and Bradley Cox, "Rationalizing Neglect: An Institutional Response to Transfer Students," *Journal of Higher Education* 83, no. 3 (May 2012): 389–410.

21. "Important Changes in the 2021 Goldwater Competition," Barry Goldwater Scholarship and Excellence in Education Foundation. Each year, the Goldwater Foundation publishes changes for the current

application cycle. (The notes for 2021 are no longer available, but for an example of such changes, see https://goldwaterscholarship.gov/new-for -2024/.)

22. "Diversity, Equity, Inclusion, and Accessibility," Fulbright US Student Program, https://us.fulbrightonline.org/about/diversity-inclusion.

5

Exploring Diversity, Equity, and Inclusion Issues for Scholarship Offices

A Personal Journey

KAREN WEBER

Overseeing a fellowships office presents a wide array of rewards and challenges. Given the complexity of the field, the many ways in which offices are constituted, and the varied roles advisors and their offices serve on campus, there is no one-size-fits-all approach to running a scholarship unit.

I have had the privilege of advising students on nationally competitive scholarships since 2004. I have worked at two state institutions—one in Texas and one in Illinois—and now work at a private institution in North Carolina. The two prior fellowships offices were housed in honors colleges; my current office is under the provost's division. All three offices have varied greatly regarding the number of students and applicants supported, the stakeholders involved in operations, and the opportunities and problems that arise accordingly.

For many years of my career, admittedly, I was not focused on issues pertaining to diversity, equity, and inclusion (DEI) nearly as much as I should have been. I tried to recruit broadly and aspired to treat my students equitably, but I was not considering the deeper DEI work that is critical when overseeing scholarship initiatives. For the past four years, I have been charged with overseeing merit scholarships and nationally competitive scholarships at Duke University. During the first few weeks of my position in the fall of 2019, my team suggested we offer diversity trainings for students and staff members.

These initial trainings opened the door to the complexities that arise when considering and offering DEI programming. As for many others, it was the racial reckoning of summer 2020 that was a call to action for me to commit and focus on the work I needed to do for my students and colleagues. It shined a spotlight on the policies, procedures, and practices I simply took for granted that required scrutiny and in many cases revision.

The irony of a middle-aged white woman named Karen writing an essay about DEI is not lost on me. I reap the benefits of many privileges, but I try to own this and in turn address inequities and act as an ally for less advantaged colleagues and students. My goal for this essay is to share the work our office has done to promote DEI work and to illustrate some of the steps we have taken in the past few years. We found these critical as we strove toward administering equitable scholarship programs. The ideas discussed and the questions raised at the end of this essay are just a starting point. Other fellowships advisors and leaders in the field (including some in this volume of essays) will be able to expand and refine these ideas, and many already have. Nevertheless, these nascent discussions are important for enhancing and expanding our work.

Overview

Overseeing a fellowships office and serving as a scholarship advisor is an unusual position in the field of higher education, providing an opportunity to work with highly motivated and talented students as they ambitiously pursue competitive programs and scholarships. Scholarship advisors collaborate with faculty and staff from across the university, including colleagues in the graduate and professional colleges. The role can interface with the provost's office, president's office, communications, financial aid, advancement, admissions, the academic colleges, general counsel, and many other units. These multiple intersections and connections present needs and challenges that many of our colleagues, such as departmental academic advisors and cocurricular coordinators, do not encounter. Scholarship advisors must stay attuned to the needs of their universities, academic colleges, and specific campus units, as well as the broader priorities in local communities and cities, in addition to state and national politics.

And then there are the students. We are contending with the digital age and the perks and pitfalls that come with working with iGen or Generation Z students, students born between 1995 and 2012.[1] For instance, until its recent rise to fame, most advisors had never heard of ChatGPT, let alone been concerned about whether to include an AI checker policy as part of the application process. In addition to evolving technological challenges, students' expectations of administrators and programs have changed. Simply put, students expect full transparency and do not tolerate injustices: "From LGBT identities to gender to race, iGen'ers expect equality and are often surprised, even shocked, to still encounter prejudice."[2] By putting processes in place to review our practices, policies, and programs, advisors can better understand how well we are living up to our inclusivity goals and identify areas for improvement. As someone who has overseen fellowship processes and units for nearly twenty years, I continually try to remind myself to delve deeper and think more critically, prompted by questions like the following:

- *How can I be more effective and equitable?*
- *What should I be considering that I am not?*
- *What am I focusing on that is no longer relevant?*
- *Where are my blind spots?*

In this essay, I share the development and implementation of the Excellence, Diversity, Inclusion, and Equity (EDIE) plan at the Office of University Scholars and Fellows (OUSF) at Duke University. Although the EDIE plan supports the entire office, including both the merit scholarship programs and the nationally competitive scholarship programs, I have primarily focused on the nationally competitive scholarship aspects of our plan. I have included information on recruitment, outreach, programming, our student advisory committee, and general counsel, as well as some examples of my own personal work in this field. This essay is intended to encourage new advisors to explore and expand on these topics as well as consider related topics not addressed here. Seasoned advisors may come away with a DEI idea to incorporate into an existing operation or can develop an approach that is more directed to their institution's DEI experiences and practices.

Development of EDIE

In October 2020, OUSF launched its inaugural EDIE plan. OUSF supports merit scholarships, nationally competitive scholarships, and other scholar programs on campus such as the Mellon Mays Undergraduate Fellowship. Our plan had to address the needs of our entire student community. We collaborated and created the plan with our OUSF team members, faculty directors, campus partners and leaders, and students—poring over each iteration of the document together. The exercise of developing and writing this plan was fruitful, allowing our team to think critically about the operation and the improvements we needed to make going forward.

In October 2021, we submitted a report on the progress of our EDIE plan to the OUSF community, which includes the students, faculty, and staff who affiliate with our office, as well as posted the executive summary on the OUSF website. We felt it was important to update the OUSF community on our efforts and where we were headed. By developing this progress report, we again had the opportunity to collaborate with colleagues across campus, such as affiliates with the cultural and identity centers and Office for Institutional Equity; clarify our goals; and analyze the status of our initiatives. We were also able to interview the students on the EDIE Student Advisory Committee to gather their feedback on the initiative and to garner their ideas on how we might move forward.

Overall, our EDIE plan has been instrumental in focusing our unit's goals, objectives, programming, and resources toward promoting a more inclusive culture. It provides a framework for us to think creatively about our operation and how we might expand our services to reach a broader population of students and faculty. Through this plan, we are consistently reviewing our practices, policies, and programs to ensure we are creating robust opportunities and multiple pathways for the OUSF community to participate in our offerings. Of course, our work in this area is far from over. We recently completed our latest progress report, which was disseminated to the OUSF community and featured on the OUSF website in the fall of 2023.

What EDIE Entails

For the purposes of this essay, I will highlight the key points of the initiative that directly pertain to nationally competitive scholarships (Figure 5.1). In our plan, the office made a commitment to do the following:

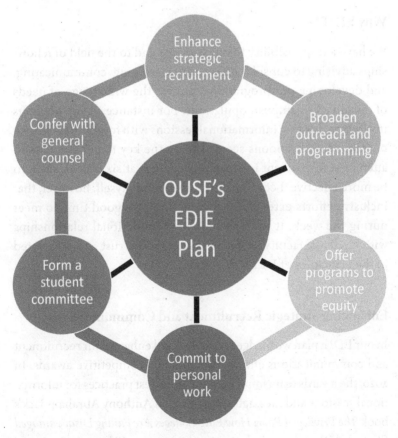

Figure 5.1. Key components of OUSF's EDIE plan.

- Enhance strategic recruitment to increase awareness of nationally competitive scholarship programs and deadlines.
- Broaden our outreach and programming.
- Offer programs to promote racial and social equity.
- Form a student advisory committee to support the plan.

Although it was not part of our initial plan, I have also included some information on the individual work we have done to educate ourselves personally. There is also a section on offering scholarship applicant waivers and working with general counsel. Considering legal issues is another step to ensure we are treating our students equitably and working in accordance with our campuses' policies.

Why EDIE?

We have a responsibility to our students and to the field of fellowships advising to consider how we are messaging, communicating, and developing our programing to meet the wide range of needs of our diverse campus populations. For instance, at my previous institution, hosting informational sessions with food at four o'clock on Thursday afternoons seemed to be the key to get students to attend. At my current institution, evenings at six o'clock seem to be more effective. I continually must remind myself, however, that inclusive efforts extend way beyond finding a good time to meet during the week. It is about building foundational relationships with students, faculty, and staff that embody trust and are rooted in the principles of DEI.

Enhancing Strategic Recruitment and Communications

In our EDIE plan we pledged to review and enhance our recruitment and communications efforts for nationally competitive awards. In 2020, the awards team implemented some best practices for informational sessions and messaging suggested in Anthony Abraham Jack's book *The Privileged Poor: How Elite Colleges Are Failing Disadvantaged Students*.[3] We determined ways in which we could be more inclusive in communications and policies. For instance, we simplified step-by-step guidelines on specific scholarships, which are available on the website for potential candidates. Also, during the pandemic, we curated a library of online video resources for Duke's community and beyond.

A new director and coordinator of scholarships in the office are exploring additional ways to recruit candidates equitably. This has compelled our team to again analyze our messaging practices—from emails to web pages to informational sessions—to ensure we are optimizing the ways in which we communicate to students. Many of the enhancements we have made have involved providing more guidance, direction, and structure to directly adhere to Gen Z students' needs.[4]

Communications with Gen Z

The traditional means of sending mass emails to invite students to events is becoming antiquated. Email feels like a tool from the past for many Gen Z students. They can view it as a formal mode of communication that takes too much time to receive a response.[5] Texting is the prominent mode of communication for Gen Z students.[6] In addition, Gen Z students are online more than any other previous generation, which includes a lot of time on Instagram and TikTok. It is certainly important for us to communicate using the university's official channels—that is, email—but publicizing informational sessions and deadlines via social media and TV screens throughout campus can be much more effective. Regardless of the mode of communication, however, keeping messaging succinct is essential.

Our OUSF team relies on our university's best practices for guidance on how to effectively use social media.[7] Building relationships with our marketing and communications offices on campus has proved fruitful. One member of our team is also affiliated with the Office of Undergraduate Education's antiracist communications committee. Since OUSF is a unit under the Office of Undergraduate Education, this committee's resources and trainings have also informed our communications.

The upside of using social media campaigns is the ability to fine-tune the analytics. For instance, our office uses Hootsuite to schedule our social media posts and to track online traffic. Since this is not my area of expertise, I lean on other staff members who are much more knowledgeable about such tools to plan our campaigns and track our effectiveness. Financially constrained offices can employ a graduate student or a savvy undergraduate either hourly or through the work-study program. Though we use social media more for our campus's merit scholarship programs currently, our plan is to increase social media use for nationally competitive scholarships in the coming years.

Broadening Outreach and Programming

The spaces in which we work, research, study, and gather on campus are an important and coveted resource and can define the ways we interact and connect with one another. This is certainly true for fellowships offices. Where they are physically and organizationally located on campus is vital to how they will be utilized and perceived.

Be that as it may, most of us have little to no say in where our offices are or will be located. Regardless of where an office is located, it is critical that we are meeting the students where they are. This is why in our EDIE plan we committed to broadening our outreach to students. For advisement sessions, this can mean taking the show on the road—traveling across campus to meet students for coffee, hosting open hours in the residence hall lounges, and offering shared sessions with the career or study abroad offices. Simply speaking, we cannot expect the campus to come to us. Currently, my office is in a remote location, so our director has created robust programming to ensure we are making ourselves readily available to students. This has included hosting the following events:

- One-hour standing appointments online each week for open advising sessions
- Advisement sessions in the residence halls, cultural and identity centers, and the library

- A Zoom option and an in-person option for one-on-one advisement appointments through Calendly, an automated scheduling software program
- Visits to student clubs and scholarship cohorts during their already-scheduled meetings

It can be hard for offices to determine whether they are meeting and reaching an optimal number of students. Learning how an awards advising office compares with similar units, such as the career, advising, and study abroad centers, can help an advisor measure how the total number of advisement appointments or students reached compares with the metrics for other units on the campus.

Offering Programs to Promote Racial and Social Equity

Before launching our EDIE plan, our office's programs ran the gamut from faculty research presentations to ice cream socials in the quad for our merit scholars. During the process of developing an EDIE plan, we examined all these programs and activities. Using Priya Parker's *The Art of Gathering* as our guide, our team questioned the purpose of each of our programs and explored how and where we gather as well as whom we are inviting to join us and by what means.[8] This was an opportunity to identify what we were trying to achieve through each of our programs. Ultimately, we decided to offer more programs that promote equity.

This led to the launch of a new event: Faculty Flash Talks on Race and Society. We invite four panelists from a variety of academic disciplines to present on their research for a total of five minutes each (hence the "flash"). Then the panelists participate in Q&A sessions to address questions from our merit scholars. Last year's topic was Black excellence in the arts; this year's topic will be environmental justice.

This successful series evolved into our office's Critical Conversations series. Now, four times each year, we invite faculty from a wide range of departments to serve on a panel to discuss issues such as health disparities and innovations in science. We folded Faculty Flash Talks into the Critical Conversations series; it is now one of the four panel sessions we host each year. The series has allowed us to collaborate with a diverse group of faculty members from across campus, as well as explore complex twenty-first-century issues with students. These lectures expose our advisors to cutting-edge research; the topics presented often provide us with material we can use in candidate interviews.

Personal Commitment to DEI

When committing to DEI efforts, an individual or personal investment is essential. For this reason, our office has coordinated a DEI book club for over three years. Our activities have ranged from studying the history of slavery to exploring identity politics to reading novels such as *The Other Black Girl* and *Such a Fun Age*. This club heightens our accountability and has also brought us closer together as a team. In *The Four Pivots: Reimagining Justice, Reimagining Ourselves*, Shawn Ginwright argues that we cannot make the transformational change we wish to make in our organizations if our interactions with our team members are transactional.[9] These types of gatherings pave the way for transformational change.

Our book club's resources also directly inform our professional work. When our team read Felicia Rose Chavez's *The Anti-racist Writing Workshop: How to Decolonize the Creative Classroom*, we were inspired by her theory of critical consciousness. We were delighted when she agreed to facilitate an online workshop for us so we could further instill her theory into our scholarship advising practice.[10] Through Chavez's model, we have learned to more effectively implement the process depicted in Figure 5.2.

Podcasts and audiobooks are important resources as well. A trip to the store, a commute to work, and a walk through the neighborhood are ideal times to catch up on pressing topics through audio resources. National Public Radio's *Codeswitch*, resources by Ashleigh Shelby Rosette, Brené Brown's *Dare to Lead*, and Adam Grant's *WorkLife* have greatly informed the way I prioritize my DEI efforts. Our campuses are also great places to stay informed. Taking time to attend lectures and forums can help sharpen our perspectives on

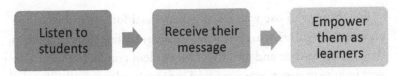

Figure 5.2. Graphic that OUSF created to explain Chavez's model on how to empower students through critical consciousness.

various issues and fields while at the same time building stronger relationships with faculty across campus.

Developing a Student Advisory Committee

One outcome of our EDIE plan was the formation of the EDIE Student Advisory Committee. These students have been helpful to our efforts, offering suggestions on communications, recruitment, and publicity. By way of example, our office used to feature photos of our scholarship recipients along our hallways with their professional headshots. The student committee members felt these photos were intimidating, and they suggested we instead feature scholars in action—conducting research, relaxing on campus, serving in the community, and so on. These action photos now fill our office walls and have contributed to a more inviting office culture. The advisory committee has implored us to be more conscientious about whose photos we are featuring and how. In short, if advisors are unsure of how to effectively message to and showcase students, ask them!

Legal Considerations

Recognizing the importance of treating all our students equally, it is prudent to consider the waivers and Family Educational Rights and Privacy Act forms we typically ask candidates to sign. Many fellowships offices require candidates to sign waivers if they are applying for a nationally competitive award. These waivers can include stipulations for applicants, such as waiving their right to view their letters, including institutional endorsements, as well as attesting that they are in good academic and disciplinary standing with the university.

For those who use waivers, it is beneficial for a member of the university's legal team to review the waiver every few years to confirm they are up-to-date and effective. Our student conduct office is also very helpful in ensuring we are working in accordance with what the university requires and expects from academic units. These conversations and document reviews help us ensure we are asking all our candidates—current students and alumni—to take the same steps and undergo the same processes when applying for scholarships. Whatever the policy is in the office, it should treat everyone the same. To ensure this, it is advisable to contact the legal counsel office.

The approval to use a student's likeness also varies from campus to campus. Some universities ask for students' approval upon admissions and this consent carries forth throughout their academic careers; others ask that program coordinators gain permission from students when using their image on websites and for social media purposes. For instance, on our campus, we ask our scholarship recipients if we can publicize their award and have them review their image in advance of publication. However, other campuses assume that this approval is a given. Again, whatever the policy is for the unit, it should be the same for all students and alumni.

Next Steps

This year's EDIE plan will align with Duke's Climate Commitment and have an environmental justice focus. We plan to promote and attend events through the Nicholas Institute for Energy, Environment and Sustainability and the Environmental Justice Lab. Our Critical Conversations series will focus on climate change; the Faculty Flash Talks on Race and Society will be on environmental justice. We also plan to heighten our recruitment efforts through the Nicholas School for programs such as the Udall and Goldwater Scholarships.

Conclusion

Creating, implementing, and assessing our EDIE plan with the OUSF team has been one of the highlights of my tenure at Duke, and I am hopeful we can continue to enhance and expand this plan in the years to come. This initiative has anchored and framed our work as we aspire to oversee scholarship programs that foster a sense of belonging for our community.

As mentioned at the beginning of this essay, I hope that by sharing some of the ways we have implemented our EDIE plan, I have provided tips and examples that will be helpful to advisors in their work. I have also included reflection questions in the appendix, which could be useful in the process. As we continue to work together to ensure our campuses are inviting and open to our students and community members, sharing our practices and lessons learned will enable us to map the best paths going forward. These initiatives promote inclusiveness and make progress toward creating the kind of transformational change we know is possible.

Appendix

Questions to Consider on Strategic Recruitment
and Communications

1. Are the students I am working with representative of the entire campus population?
2. Do I know how my students prefer to be contacted and messaged?
3. Do I have the data I need to make informed decisions about messaging?
4. Do I have the campus contacts I need to make informed decisions about messaging?
5. Does my website adhere to the ever-changing needs of my users, specifically Gen Z populations?
6. Would my office benefit from relying more on social media?
7. If so, do I have the resources and expertise to use it effectively?

Questions to Consider on Broadening Outreach
and Programming

8. Would I like more students to schedule appointments with me?
9. If so, where are convenient locations on campus to meet them?

10. If so, whom could I ally with on campus to host open advisement hours or an info session at peak student times?
11. Do I have the technology I need to effectively host and manage virtual appointments?
12. Do I know how my office compares with similar units, such as the career, advising, and study abroad centers, regarding student visitations?

Questions to Consider on Offering Programs to Promote Equity

13. Are there ways to modify my current programs to promote equity more fully?
14. Do my programs effectively engage students and faculty in ways that promote DEI and antiracist dialogues?
15. Are there lectures or events on campus that promote equity that I can support through attending their events or cohosting activities?

Questions to Consider on Personal Commitment to DEI

16. How am I currently committing to my personal DEI efforts?
17. Are there ways I might focus or enhance my efforts?
18. Are there friends, family members, or colleagues who might wish to share my commitment to heighten my accountability?

Questions to Consider on Legal Issues

19. What does good standing mean at my institution?
20. Should a waiver be required from candidates?
21. If so, when in the application process should it be required?
22. Which people on my campus have the privilege to review candidates' applications?
23. Should I get permission from recipients to publicize their award?
24. If so, how will this permission be attained?

25. If the press release includes a photo, will the recipient need to approve the photo before publication?
26. If so, how will this permission be attained?

Notes

1. Jean M. Twenge, *iGen: Why Today's Super-connected Kids Are Growing Up Less Rebellious, More Tolerant, Less Happy—and Completely Unprepared for Adulthood (and What This Means for the Rest of Us)* (New York: Atria Books, 2017), 6.
2. Twenge, 226.
3. Anthony Abraham Jack, *The Privileged Poor: How Elite Colleges Are Failing Disadvantaged Students* (Cambridge, MA: Harvard University Press, 2019).
4. Jean M. Twenge, *Generations: The Real Difference between Gen Z, Millennials, Gen X, Boomers, and Silents—and What They Mean for America's Future* (New York: Atria Books, 2023).
5. Corey Seemiller and Meghan Grace, *Generation Z Goes to College* (San Francisco: John Wiley and Sons, 2016), 60.
6. Seemiller and Grace, 58.
7. "Social Media Guidelines," Duke Communicator Toolkit, https://communicators.duke.edu/multimedia/social-media-guidelines-for-communicators/.
8. Priya Parker, *The Art of Gathering: How We Meet and Why It Matters* (New York: Riverhead Books, 2018).
9. Shawn Ginwright, *The Four Pivots: Reimagining Justice, Reimagining Ourselves* (Berkeley: North Atlantic Books, 2022), 99.
10. Felicia Rose Chavez, *The Anti-racist Writing Workshop: How to Decolonize the Creative Classroom* (Chicago: Haymarket Books, 2021).

6

Connecting and Supporting Historically Marginalized Students

Access, Opportunity, and Empowerment

ELIZABETH ROTOLO

When I first started at Brandeis University, I was excited to join in one of those catch-all roles that are common across higher education. Over the first few years, I was responsible for a 3 + 2 engineering agreement, an undergraduate research fellowship that was cycling out, and a scholarship program for underrepresented students that was in desperate need of some structure. The other half of my job was advising for nationally competitive awards. I was in the midst of a career transition out of student affairs and had the rare opportunity to try out multiple units across academic affairs with one position.

I could immediately see the benefit to having my job reach so many different corners of campus. Our fellowship applicants tended to represent more privileged identities, skewing more white identifying and less first generation. On the flip side, our Martin Luther King (MLK) Fellows, for whom I served as an academic advisor, were usually low-income, first-generation students of color. During MLK Fellow cohort meetings and events, it was easy to forget that Brandeis was a predominantly white institution as I facilitated community-building activities. As I came to know the MLK Fellows better, and simultaneously became versed in the jargon of advising for prestigious academic opportunities, I noticed a glaring disconnect. As the MLK Fellows came to trust me, they shared assumptions they had about these opportunities (e.g., "I can't afford to study abroad"; "My

GPA is below a 4.0 so I can't apply, right?") and myths that pervaded peer conversations (e.g., "There is no research in the arts"; "People who look like us don't apply for things like that"). I found myself in the curious position of serving as a coach, translator, cheerleader, and sounding board as I worked with students to tease out the barriers, real and imagined, and determine how we could broaden participation in our fellowship application processes.[1]

The comments that follow are the result of ten years of conversations, assessments, edits, and more conversations. After hours and hours of reading, writing, consulting, and presenting, my two biggest takeaways have been that the work is always evolving, and connecting and supporting historically marginalized students cannot happen in a vacuum. It takes many voices, including those of campus partners, fellow members of the National Association of Fellowships Advisors (NAFA), foundation representatives, and most importantly the applicants themselves, to help us understand our practices in a new light and to remove barriers in order to broaden participation in application processes. Building trust with the campus community, especially students, is a top priority for any advising office. When students trust that advisors value them as individuals and are working to improve inclusion efforts, they will share necessary insights to help advisors shift their lens and remove barriers that may not even have been visible to the advisor.

Critical Race Theory: What It Is and What That Teaches Us

When we zoom out to explore the systems and frameworks that affect our relationships with students, application processes, and foundations, critical race theory (CRT) provides a helpful framework for understanding systems and identities that can affect these connections. For the past few years, CRT has been a popular buzzword, used to describe a variety of topics, strategies, and curriculum items across both K–12 and higher education. When reviewing the literature, we can see that the current political landscape has co-opted a term with a much more specific origin. CRT originated as a critical analysis of race and racism from a legal point of view. The term was first officially developed in 1989, at the inaugural Workshop on Critical Race Theory, though it originated through works and discussion among Derrick Bell, Kimberlé Crenshaw, Cheryl Harris, Richard Delgado, Patricia Williams, Gloria Ladson-Billings, Tara Yosso, and others throughout the 1960s and 1970s.[2] CRT recognizes that racism is ingrained in the fabric and system of American society. An individual racist does not need to exist for institutional racism to be pervasive in our dominant culture. CRT identifies that these power structures are based on privilege, perpetuating the marginalization of people of color.

One important tenet of CRT is intersectionality. This concept, introduced by Crenshaw in an article focused specifically on Black women, explores the complex way the effects of multiple forms of discrimination (such as racism and sexism) combine and overlap to shape the experiences of marginalized individuals.[3] Crenshaw's work outlines the multidimensionality of oppressions and recognizes that race alone cannot account for the disempowerment of a person or a group. In other words, when meeting with a student, the racial identity of the student and the advisor do not necessarily determine the experience for either party. For a student to feel emotionally safe, equitably supported, and empowered, advisors should consider the multiple active and passive messages that are present in their office. CRT explores the many oppressions facing people of color and does not allow for a one-dimensional approach to understanding and addressing the complexities of our world.

This can feel overwhelming, especially in a field made up of one-person offices, ad hoc assignments, and an additional influx of postpandemic personal and professional challenges. CRT fortunately also provides a suggested antidote—personal narratives, or counterstories, that center the experiences of people of color. These stories complicate and "challenge the story of white supremacy and continue to give a voice to those that have been silenced by white supremacy."[4] They challenge the notion of meritocracy as colorblind or "value neutral." This is where I find the most joy in fellowships advising. It offers a student the chance to be seen and heard—by me, by application readers, by interview committees, and more. Our institutions are continuing to increase conversations about diversity, equity, inclusion, and belonging as demographics change across newly admitted classes and campuses respond to the recent Supreme Court ruling to end race-conscious college admissions. Allowing students a safe place to workshop their personal narratives provides a meaningful tool to enhance self-confidence, combat privilege, and increase accessibility across identities.

Culturally Responsive Advising

Building relationships is at the core of the recruitment, retention, and persistence of college students. Students are looking for personal and meaningful relationships with adults they trust. While this can include faculty and staff members who share identities, that is not always a prerequisite for a mentoring relationship. In fact, forced identity-based mentoring matches can have unintended negative consequences if the mentor (or mentee) feels they are being reduced to a single aspect of their identity. As Blane Harding observes, "It is not necessary to look like the students we advise, but it is mandatory that we gain their respect and in turn give them the respect they deserve.... Advisors must ... let students choose what aspects of their identity are important to them at any given time. Students, just like the rest of us in society, go in and out of identities given the situations and people they find themselves around."[5]

This requires a delicate balance when it comes to recruitment, advising, and especially publicity. Where a student falls in their racial identity development[6] may heavily influence how they respond to the marketing and eligibility criteria for a specific opportunity. For example, a Black student who is in the "dissonance and appreciating" phase might be actively looking for opportunities that expressly welcome and support applicants who identify as Black. Another Black student, one in the "resistance and immersion" phase, may be unreceptive to being categorized and further assume that the advisor's targeted suggestions are an example of institutionalized racist structures. If we are using racially informed eligibility criteria to make identity-specific suggestions, we run the risk of alienating some students who are sensitive to being reduced to one identity, especially if that identity is not one that is salient for them in their current stage of identity development. Conversely, shying away from naming identity in an advising conversation is a missed developmental opportunity for the applicant, and it does a disservice to students who might be eligible for a particular award.

So what is an advisor to do when, for example, one Black student is only interested in opportunities that are explicitly designed to support Black excellence, and the next Black student to enter the office is offended that the advisor has reduced them to their skin color, especially if their gender identity or religion is a more salient identity for that individual? Culturally responsive advising practices direct us to be mindful of the passive and active messages that are communicated in our words, our physical spaces, and our marketing communications. As Eric G. Carnaje states, "It is . . . about understanding the way in which institutions and . . . offices become racialized spaces, spaces that are historically and politically charged in concept and physicality. For example, academic advising sessions that occur in an open, non-private room or area may suggest to the student of Color that it is unsafe or unwise to discuss personal matters or challenges related to his or her racial identity."[7]

We cannot anticipate how each individual person will react to us or our office space. We can, however, work to be clear and consistent with our communication to minimize that which can be left up to interpretation. Trauma-informed practices[8] highlight the importance of offering applicants as much control as possible (e.g., offering in-person and virtual meetings, allowing students to decide if meetings are held with the door open or closed, sharing a rough agenda before or at the beginning of the meeting so they know what to expect). When meeting with a new student, we cannot know their past experiences with or their expectations of authority figures. Many applicants seek out our office for access to our expertise. They see us as the holders of important knowledge, be it of available opportunities or chances to network with foundation representatives and past recipients, or simply as professional adults who are older and wiser. For other students, especially those with historically marginalized identities, authority figures may have played a very different role in their lives. Current newspaper headlines are peppered with stories of police brutality, politicians rolling back protections, and educational inequities at all levels. For many students on our campuses, an authority figure is someone not to be trusted, and approaching our offices is an emotional risk in its own right. Culturally responsive advising directs us to understand that our virtual and physical offices are not a neutral space, and we must actively work to reduce barriers, real and perceived, in order to allow all students to engage with us on their own terms.

Language Matters: It's Okay to Be Uncomfortable

One theme throughout this essay will be that language matters. The language we choose, in our individual conversations, in our marketing materials, in our assessments, and so on, shapes the ways that both our students and our colleagues understand our roles as fellowships advisors and which students we serve. One of the most important, and often most difficult, practices when we are designing inclusive communications is to "say what you mean and mean what you say."

For example, when our campus references "underrepresented" students, which students are we referring to? Do we mean students of color? And if so, why is it uncomfortable to name that? Perhaps we mean students of color or BIPOC (Black, Indigenous, and other people of color) students, or first-generation or low-income students? Do we mean students who were historically excluded from higher education? Once words like *marginalized* or *historically excluded* are present in the conversation, things can become tense depending on the stakeholders in the room. However, by becoming more comfortable with accurately naming what we mean, we can more meaningfully work to reach our goals.

For example, if we want to "recruit more underrepresented applicants," it will be important to distinguish how and why Black students may have different needs from Latinx students, which may or may not overlap with the needs of our transgender or low-income students. It is important to hold space for individuals, and not to view identity groups as monoliths. By using precise language, disaggregating data, and honoring individual needs, we can build trust with the campus community as a whole, which will ultimately lead to improved experiences for all applicants. By building processes and procedures that are transparent and inclusive from the ground up, we can remove barriers for all applicants, regardless of identity.

Conducting a Self-Audit

It is important to acknowledge that there are many forces involved in every stage of every competition. Fellowships advisors cannot control the language used on a campus partner's or foundation's website. The institution's communications office may choose to publicize (or not) a student story. A foundation may cap the number of nominees per campus. A colleague may hold back a referral to prevent overloading an already stressed student or out of fear of setting them up for disappointment. While it can be easy to get sidetracked by outside influences, there is also power in focusing on what is within an advisor's sphere of control.

I have found it helpful to set aside time for a self-audit. This could occur over the summer, as part of an office's annual review or annual reporting process, or in the offseason from your most time-intensive processes (i.e., not in September). Offices, campuses, and student bodies are all different, so I have outlined in the following sections a series of questions to consider, broken up into different categories, each with a different level of control. To start, consider the space where advising offices (hopefully) have a good deal of autonomy.

Your Physical and Virtual Office: "Can I Find You, and If I Do, Do I Feel Comfortable in Your Office?"

Prospective applicants can be introduced to our offices in many ways. They may see a post featuring a friend in their Instagram or LinkedIn feed. Our website might pop up in a Google search, or they could be referred by a professor. If an office is located in a high-traffic area, perhaps the potential candidate sees the physical door first and stops to ask, "What is a fellowships office?"

When examining these many options for first impressions, it is important to consider how easy the office is to find, and how welcoming the spaces feel. Some questions to consider include the following:

- Where is the office physically located on campus?
- Is the office website fully accessible?
- Are the office's social media pages fully accessible?
- Who is represented in images used by the office?
- How easy is it to schedule an appointment?
- What is on the door?
- What is in the office (e.g., pictures, flyers, posters, books, diplomas)?

While advisors might not be able to select their physical location on campus, they can be thoughtful about how a student experiences a trip to the office. Is the office in a heavily trafficked student center filled with natural light and impromptu student meetings? Is it the last door in the basement hallway with no discernible room number? Is it tucked away within an honors college or specific academic department where nonhonors or nonmajor students might not know how to find it? Is the office accessible to those with mobility challenges? Is there more than one way to contact the office? Each office and campus will have a different preference for meeting schedulers, intake forms, individual emails, and responses to social media messages, but allowing students different modes of accessing the office with minimal barriers will broaden access to those who might be less familiar with a particular technology or intimidated by a multistep process.

At Brandeis we recently had the rare privilege of relocating to a new office space, which allowed our team to tackle these questions with a blank slate. We selected comfortable, colorful furniture for our welcome area and ordered prints of our student advice social media campaign to place on the walls.[9] A number of students have popped by after seeing a friend's picture from the hallway and have come in to inquire about our office. Within our individual offices, we took time to be intentional with decorations and personal items to give the space a comfortable feel. I have a collection of stuffed animals from past student leaders that always draws attention during intake appointments. Especially for students who are unsure about whether they are a "worthy" applicant, humanizing the space can decrease anxiety and open conversations.

Marketing and Recruitment: "What Are the Implicit Messages I'm Receiving?"

Many of our foundation partners offer fantastic marketing materials, and it is our job as advisors to tailor our outreach to our particular campus population. This can require a delicate, nuanced approach as we navigate the desire to encourage students to put themselves out there while also knowing the competitive odds of these programs are never in the applicant's favor. It is important to consider how we are both actively and passively marketing what makes a "successful" fellowship applicant, as well as how we are navigating the sensitive topic of finances. Some questions to consider include the following:

- How are we reaching out to students?
- What do our meeting invitations look like?
- Is the language in printed materials accessible to everyone?
- Are we acknowledging the financial component and possible impacts on financial aid?
- What photos and other images do we use in our materials?

One of my favorite examples is the term RSVP. From campus events to weddings to children's birthday parties, this is a common acronym with a general understanding that a reply is requested to confirm attendance. But how many people know the origin of the term? RSVP originated from the French phrase *répondez s'il vous plaît* (respond please). A quick Google search reveals that this phrase is too archaic and too formal for regular use among French speakers. This leads me to wonder, if it is not used regularly in its original language, is it fair to assume that all corners of American life, including all socioeconomic demographics, are familiar with this term?

Beyond the United States, can we assume that all of our international students who speak English as a second language have been taught old, French-based acronyms in their English language instruction? What about adaptive technology—do screen readers differentiate between "RSVP" and "R.S.V.P."?

I do not claim to know the answers to these questions myself, and I would agree it is quite tedious to engage in this level of detective work for every acronym we come across. But there is another, much more inclusive, solution. Rather than asking students to "RSVP" for events, which assumes a specific set of cultural and linguistic capital, we can eliminate the jargon and offer the straightforward request, including the desired action step. Saying instead, "sign up through the following link" or "reserve your seat by filling out this form" removes the guesswork for the student and moves us closer to the conversation we are looking to have. Removing jargon signals to all applicants that there is not a minimum level of cultural capital required to cross the threshold of my office. Especially for first-generation and low-income college students, this is an important step to help mitigate applicants self-selecting out before they even begin a process.

Another important piece to consider is the financial impact of these awards. As higher education becomes increasingly expensive, there is intense pressure for many students to find additional funding sources at all degree levels. While we hope each fellowship application process is reflective and developmental for every applicant, the hard truth is that for some the financial assistance will be a necessary and primary motivator. This is not inherently negative given the size and prestige of some of the awards in our portfolio, but it does make a rejection letter more difficult to digest if a student is in need of additional funds to remain in school or secure an advanced degree.

Over the years, our team has built a strong relationship with the financial aid office to help anticipate and communicate impacts of external scholarships on financial aid packages. While advising the MLK Fellows, I worked with a number of students who were successful in national award competitions. The MLK Fellowship included a full-need scholarship, which covered the fellow's tuition and fees beyond their calculated expected family contribution (EFC). For many, this amounted to a full-ride scholarship, and for others their EFC could be covered by loans or personal funds. What the students often did not initially realize was that many outside scholarships would replace MLK funding, rather than be applied to their EFC or be issued as a check directly to the student.

I remember one student in particular who was thrilled to receive a national scholarship toward her study abroad experience. Mere days before boarding the plane, she realized that while she had expected a check from the funding organization, the funds were instead sent directly to Brandeis and simply replaced part of her MLK award. I had not realized this mismatch in expectations until my very upset recipient sent a series of very angry emails. Collaborating with campus partners, we were able to work within federal financial aid guidelines to ensure there was an overall net benefit to the student. In her case we were lucky to have some tools at our disposal; different campuses may have internal policies that provide more or less flexibility. In our enthusiasm for helping students to dream big and reflect through writing, we may be tempted to separate the realities of the financial implications from the value of the application process itself. Taking the time to be thoughtful in the marketing language and creating space to have frank conversations about monetary impacts can remove unfortunate surprises later in the process. Especially when working with applicants on awards that provide undergraduate scholarship funds (e.g., Gilman, Udall, Boren), having a knowledgeable partner in the university's financial aid office is an incredible asset.

The Campus Application Process: "Does the Process Feel Fair and Welcoming?"

Regardless of the final outcome, every applicant should feel that the application process was managed in a fair and transparent manner. Since decisions and processes at the national level are outside the control of the advisor, it is that much more important that students can trust the process at the campus level. For applicants with historically marginalized identities, a campus application process can help to demystify the hidden curriculum of applications and prepare them to search for and apply for opportunities strategically in the future. The following are a few questions to consider when reviewing your internal processes:

- What barriers are there in the process?
- Is the language clear and inclusive at every step of the process?
- Where might there be "hidden curriculum" or "unwritten rules"?

Barriers to entry can occur at any stage and are often disguised as useful tools intended to streamline the process. For example, many campuses use "intake" or "intent to apply" forms. These can provide helpful information to direct an initial conversation with a student, collect demographic data, keep track of a large applicant pool, serve as a prewriting exercise, and more. However, without context, these tools can also serve as a barrier to approaching the office.

Many campuses include various demographic data in their intake forms (e.g., class year, major, identity, citizenship, GPA). For advisors, this is very helpful information to have ahead of a meeting to ensure that they advise students to consider awards for which they are eligible. It is always deeply uncomfortable to manifest enthusiasm for an opportunity that the advisor then has to walk back because the student does not meet the eligibility criteria, particularly if it is related to part of the applicant's identity (such as citizenship). Well intended as demographic questions are, they also leave open the opportunity for interpretation from the student. For international or undocumented students, a question about citizenship may lead them to assume this is a "weed-out" question, and they may leave the form uncompleted. A humanities student whose early dabbling in the prehealth curriculum went poorly may see the GPA question and assume their first-semester chemistry grade renders them not competitive for national awards. For first-generation, low-income, and BIPOC students, imposter syndrome is a pervasive issue, and these questions open the door for them to self-select out before even setting foot in our offices.

Depending on the size of the institution and scope of the advisor's role, adding structure such as intake forms may be necessary to manage workflow. So how does one find a compromise between these conflicting needs? One way to mitigate student assumptions is to add clarifying language whenever possible. For example, for our internal "intent to apply" forms, we always include an eligibility section, which provides both an eligibility check for us and education for the students. For our current Fulbright Intent to Apply Form, the eligibility section includes the following header: "You can see the full list of official and 'preferred' eligibility criteria on the Fulbright Website: https://us.fulbrightonline.org/about/eligibility. Please note that certain countries may list additional requirements in the country summary. You are welcome to contact the Academic Fellowships Team if you have any questions regarding the specific criteria for your intended program." The first question is a yes/no checkbox asking whether the applicant is a US citizen. This question is followed by the text, "There are other fellowship opportunities open to non-US citizens. Please be in touch with the Academic Fellowships Team if you would like more information about those options." This structure allows our team to clarify that (1) the eligibility criteria are set by the funding organization rather than our office, (2) if a student does not meet the citizenship eligibility criteria for this award, we are still open to talking with them about other opportunities, and (3) we acknowledge that the selection criteria are not always clear-cut (we have a follow-up question about dual citizenship) and we are open to questions.

Taking this approach to all passive materials (forms, websites, social media, brochures, handouts, etc.) can reduce the barriers that applicants encounter throughout the process. Explaining the difference between a "recommendation" and a "reference," allowing students to openly self-identify for demographic data (rather than checkboxes), clarifying dress code requirements (or eliminating them all together), and proactively offering accommodations for meetings and interviews are all practices that can help applicants feel that they are able to fully participate in the campus process. Even if they are not ultimately selected for an award, or even as a campus nominee, students can still look back on their experience with the knowledge that the process was equitable and that they learned valuable lessons about how to apply for opportunities in the future.

Campus Partners: "Do I Trust You to Hold Space for the Whole Student?"

As we have emerged from the pandemic to rebuild our cross-campus relationships, one prepandemic truth remains painfully true: not all campus partners are created equal. The work of fellowships advising cannot be done well without a robust support system across campus. Helpful collaborators can make the application process smoother and more reflective for the applicant. Unhelpful partners can unintentionally become roadblocks to our work. At best, some challenging colleagues can give advice counter to our NAFA values of meaningful self-reflection, integrity, and intellectual development (how many of us have had to coach a student to help the faculty recommender understand that the student cannot write their own letter?). At worst, an unhelpful campus partner can reinforce a student's feeling of unworthiness or even directly advise against applying for awards at the national level.

Faculty committees, career advisors, study abroad staff, writing centers, and more are necessary partners for the ecosystem of applicant advising to be successful. And yet, if I refer a student to another office that then causes harm, it has the potential to break that applicant's trust with me as well. Here are some questions to consider when reviewing new and existing campus partnerships:

- Where is the office located within the campus organization chart?
- Who has been a helpful campus partner?
- Who has been an unhelpful campus partner?
- What is the best way to build a trusted network of culturally competent referrals?
- How can fellowships advisors be helpful partners for other colleagues?

It is a common challenge for NAFA members to mitigate problematic advice from mentors, student services advisors, and others who may be trying to prevent an applicant from wasting valuable time or setting themselves up for disappointment. For students who are already well connected on campus and used to navigating conflicting advice, it is unlikely that one negative comment will cause them to drop out of a process. But for students who have a history of educational trauma, do not feel a sense of belonging on campus, or are new to navigating their community's resources, even one negative interaction can have serious consequences for their overall experience with the institution.

I choose to believe that no one who opts to work in higher education is actively seeking to do harm, and yet it is naïve to think that all of our faculty and staff members have amassed the experience and cultural competence to advise every student effectively. Many of our campuses are suffering from employee retention issues, and faculty and staff are being tasked to fill increasing gaps in services with fewer and fewer resources. Burnt-out employees are more prone to mistakes and have less time and bandwidth to manage the often complicated dynamics of challenge and support.[10]

At Brandeis, we have found it helpful to build a network of faculty and staff whom we can trust to care for the whole student. We regularly ask students which of our campus colleagues have been particularly helpful conversation partners as they utilize different offices across campus. If we make a direct referral, we follow up to ask about how the interaction went with that staff member. In recent years we have increased staff presence on our selection committees, both to bring in new expertise and to fill gaps left by overburdened faculty. By listening to who the students have found helpful and supportive, we have built new relationships across both academic affairs and student affairs. This has resulted in many successful recommendations to campus leadership programs, smooth referrals to our study abroad office, and a particular contact in our career center who has been indispensable to our Truman and Udall applicants as they explore public service careers. Building this network of consistent support for students reinforces the interdisciplinary nature of our work and helps them feel that they have the support of the community as they navigate the application process.

A Few Closing Thoughts

When thinking about diversity, equity, inclusion, and belonging on our campuses and in our offices, it is easy to become overwhelmed or discouraged. There are many competing forces at play, most of which are beyond our control. That said, there is also great power and promise in focusing on what the advisor can control and choosing to remove barriers wherever possible.

There is no one-size-fits-all model for this work. Every institution has a different student body, in a different location, with different strengths and challenges. And even if they were all the same, each advisor is a different person and brings with them different talents, skills, and lived experiences as they enter the office each day. This leads me back to my two opening points: the work is always evolving, and connecting and supporting historically marginalized students cannot happen in a vacuum.

Part of the reason that this work is so complex is that the demographics are always changing. American higher education originated with a very narrow view of who can and should be a student. As our admission practices have evolved, we have welcomed new groups of students to campus, including women, BIPOC individuals, and students with disabilities. With new identities present in each new class that arrives on campus, our resources and support strategies must adapt. Brandeis University is proud to be the first institution in the nation to recognize caste as a protected class,[11] and with that comes a responsibility to equitably support all community members regardless of caste background. We cannot know how language and identity will evolve in the coming years, but by committing to a process of ongoing learning and reflection, we can be prepared to improve the accessibility of our offices and our resources for all prospective applicants.

This work takes the efforts of the whole community. No one person can be an expert on everything, and it is irresponsible to try. By having a network of trusted campus partners, fellow advisors, and foundation partners, we can use our collective knowledge to think creatively, advocate for more equitable and transparent processes, and better advise all our applicants.

Notes

1. I want to recognize and thank the Brandeis University MLK Fellow classes of 2014–25. Your honesty, vulnerability, humor, and trust continue to influence my work daily. I am forever grateful for your insights and the ways you have shaped my practice.
2. Richard Delgado and Jean Stefancic, "Critical Race Theory: An Annotated Bibliography," *Virginia Law Review* 79, no. 2 (1993): 461–516. For additional information, see Janel George, "A Lesson on Critical Race Theory," *Human Rights Magazine,* January 11, 2021, https://www.americanbar.org/groups/crsj/publications/human_rights_magazine_home/civil-rights-reimagining-policing/a-lesson-on-critical-race-theory/.
3. Kimberlé Crenshaw, "Demarginalizing the Intersection of Race and Sex: A Black Feminist Critique of Antidiscrimination Doctrine, Feminist Theory and Antiracist Politics," *University of Chicago Legal Forum 1989* (1989): 139–167. Reprinted in *The Politics of Law: A Progressive Critique,* 2nd ed., ed. David Kairys (New York: Pantheon, 1990), 195–217.
4. "What Is Critical Race Theory?," Critical Race Studies, UCLA School of Public Affairs, https://spacrs.wordpress.com/what-is-critical-race-theory/.
5. Blane Harding, "Advising Students of Color," NACADA Clearinghouse of Academic Advising Resources, November 5, 2012, http://www.nacada.ksu.edu/Resources/Clearinghouse/View-Articles/Advising-students-of-color.aspx.
6. The literature on racial identity development is broad and continuously evolving as social and cultural influences shape how students understand themselves and others. Advisors interested in learning more about the stages of development and how they shape student experiences might consider the works of William Cross, Janet Helms, Marc Johnston-Guerrero, Kristen Renn, and Charmaine L. Wijeyesinghe.
7. Eric G. Carnaje, "Advising across Race: Providing Culturally-Sensitive Academic Advising at Predominantly White Institutions," *Vermont Connection* 37, no. 1 (2016): 42.

8. The National Center for Trauma-Informed Care lists six principles that guide a trauma-informed approach: safety, trustworthiness and transparency, peer support, collaboration and mutuality, empowerment and choice, and cultural, historical, and gender issues. For more information and an infographic, see "Infographic: 6 Guiding Principles to a Trauma-Informed Approach," Office of Readiness and Response, Centers for Disease Control and Prevention, last reviewed September 17, 2020, https://www.cdc.gov/orr/infographics/6_principles_trauma_info.htm.

9. Thank you to Meredith Monaghan for your continued support of our students, this essay, and me personally, and for your keen eye for interior design. Our suite looks wonderful and welcoming, and all of the credit goes to you.

10. Nevitt Sanford, *Where Colleges Fail: A Study of the Student as a Person* (San Francisco: Jossey-Bass, 1968).

11. See "Adding Caste to Our Non-discrimination and Harassment Policy," Office of the President, Brandeis University, December 17, 2019, https://www.brandeis.edu/president/letters/2019-12-17-adding-caste-to-our-nondiscrimination-harassment-policy.html.

7

Toward an Antiracist Fellowships Advising Model

KURT DAVIES

A t a 2003 summit of executive administrators of major fellowships programs, foundation representatives expressed a desire to attract applications from a broader and more diverse range of applicants. The participants acknowledged that traditional merit-based selection processes excluded talented students from underrepresented populations or underresourced undergraduate institutions.[1] In the last two decades, the conversation on diversity within fellowships has expanded.

Indeed, Rhodes and Marshall, two of the most well-known and prestigious postgraduate fellowship programs, have both launched initiatives to reach out to students at institutions that have produced no or few recipients. In 2022, the Association of Marshall Scholars published an outreach plan to promote the scholarship to students from historically underrepresented backgrounds and underresourced institutions.[2] As part of its recently published equity and inclusion goals, the Rhodes Trust states that it will "reach out to students from historically marginalized communities or overlooked institutions" and highlights supporting existing outreach initiatives spearheaded by the Association of American Rhodes Scholars.[3]

However, there remain existing tensions between publicly stated goals and aspirations and the actual practices employed by many of these awards programs. Indeed, in a 2022 letter to the editor of the *American Oxonian*, the secretary of the US Rhodes constituency at the time wrote, "No selector should think institutional diversity (or any other kind of diversity) should be a factor in our selections. Each committee should choose the candidate or candidates who best meet the criteria for selection—regardless of institution—just as candidates should be chosen regardless of academic field, gender, gender identity, sexual orientation, economic status, marital status, geography, disability, race, ethnic origin, ideology or partisan identification, religion, or how 'representative' they are of their state. You are to choose the strongest candidates under the criteria of the Will of Cecil Rhodes, with no balancing considerations of any kind."[4]

This letter clearly states that Rhodes selectors should judge candidates solely on their individual merits and that consideration of applicants' context, resources, and personal backgrounds should not factor into scholar selection. This admonishment points directly to the tensions involved in the diversification of higher education. Attracting increased numbers of students with a broader cross section of identities is only one step in addressing inequities within the field.

Fellowships advisors play a critical role in creating more equitable fellowships processes. In this essay, I will discuss the ways that antiracist frameworks can be used to address and dismantle oppressive systems within our field. I will then share my experience implementing one particular framework, that presented in Felicia Rose Chavez's *Anti-racist Writing Workshop*, in my own advising practice.

Positionality Statement

I am a white, queer, gender-nonconforming male. I grew up in a middle-class military family, moving every few years throughout my childhood and adolescence. My K–12 education took place in a mixture of public, Department of Defense, and private Christian schools, and I graduated high school in Ankara, Turkey. I earned my bachelor's degree from the University of North Carolina at Chapel Hill as a nontraditional student at the age of thirty. I subsequently earned a master's degree in higher education from the University of Pennsylvania and am currently a doctoral candidate in higher education administration at New York University (NYU).

I have worked in fellowships advising since 2014. I have worked at Villanova University, a private Catholic doctoral university; James

Madison University, a regional public master's-level university; and NYU, a private, very high-level research university. All three of these schools are Predominantly White Institutions (PWIs). I currently serve on the board of directors for the National Association of Fellowships Advisors.

I have received training in facilitation across differences in identity through Villanova's InterGroup Dialogue program and restorative justice training at NYU. Like most fellowships advisors, I am not formally trained in writing pedagogy or advising practice, and I have learned most of my approaches on the job.

Background

In his landmark essay, George Sefa Dei proposes a specific framework for antiracist practice in education.[5] He suggests that dismantling systemic and structural racism requires active efforts to acknowledge, engage with, and combat the manifestations of white supremacy and other oppressive cultural norms within education. Over the last three decades, in the wake of the Black Lives Matter movement and the racial reckonings of the late 2010s and early 2020s, antiracism has moved from academia into the mainstream, with myriad books on the topic by authors like Ibram X. Kendi, Robin DiAngelo, and Ijeoma Oluo becoming bestsellers.

A wide range of antiracist frameworks have been introduced in academic literature and popular discourse.[6] While there is variety in the precise steps and suggestions in each framework, several consistent themes emerge, each of which has guided my own practice: education and awareness, starting with the self; identifying manifestations of systemic racism in one's realms of engagement; being proactive; and shifting from an individual toward a community mindset.

The task of addressing systemic racism must not be left exclusively to educators of color. Given the existing power structures within higher education, wherein Whiteness dominates cultural standards and practices, it is imperative that white practitioners serve as allies to their peers and students of color.[7] Antiracist allyship involves members of the dominant culture actively working to end the privileges that they have gained from said membership.[8] As our field—like much of higher education—is disproportionately populated by white people, it is particularly necessary for us to examine our own positionality when working with students from diverse racial and ethnic backgrounds.

Of course, incorporating antiracist practice does not come without challenges. In their study of white educators in K–12 contexts, Gloria Boutte and Tambra Jackson identify three consistent barriers to antiracist practice.[9] First, white educators regularly express concerns that discussing racism can make them vulnerable to attack or critique, a concern also found by Derek Sue and colleagues and explored by Robin DiAngelo in her 2018 book *White Fragility*.[10] Second, many white educators espouse colorblind or race-neutral philosophies. Finally, white educators express concerns that internal institutional policies and politics discourage explicit engagement with race, as educators who challenge norms may be subject to punishment or retribution.

Systemic Racism in Higher Education

Systemic racism, as described by Teresa Guess, is racism that has historically evolved and currently operates at the macro levels of society.[11] Different from individual acts of racism, systemic racism includes structures, processes, and organizations whose norms and standards of behavior were built on historically racist legacies and outlooks. Examples of systemic racism in higher education include the use of standardized tests for admissions; the prioritization of European history, philosophy, and culture; and the ubiquity of the deficit model when considering students of color.[12]

Whiteness as a theoretical concept is not based on the pigmentation of skin but on the centering of cultural values, standards, and outlooks on those that have historically been espoused by European colonizers.[13] White supremacy is the implicit or explicit belief that these norms are superior to those of nonwhite populations and communities, resulting in racial subordination for nonwhite peoples.

Describing the prevalence of Whiteness in the US higher education system, Diane Gusa states, "Today's [PWIs] do not have to be explicitly racist to create a hostile environment. Instead, unexamined historically situated White cultural ideology embedded in the language, cultural practices, traditions, and perceptions of knowledge allows these institutions to remain racialized."[14]

Antiracism and Fellowships

Fellowships advisors can draw on existing antiracist frameworks to inform all areas of our practice. We must first acknowledge the manifestations of structural racism within our field. Most of the awards supported by our offices are built on the concept of meritocracy. Introduced by Michael Young in 1958, meritocracy is the idea that an individual's social and economic standing is determined by their individual effort and ability.[15] In the second half of the twentieth century, as US higher education enrollments skyrocketed, elite higher education institutions implemented selective admissions processes and a move toward holistic review practices.[16] These practices rested on the assumption that merit and future promise can be discovered by examining an applicant's full track record of engagement and attempting to determine their motivation for continued pursuit and future success.[17]

Critiques of this move toward meritocracy state that, rather than evaluating merit, these processes evaluate access to cultural capital, or experiences that demonstrate an individual's value to—and ability to operate within—the existing elite class.[18] Meritocracy, therefore, when applied inequitably in higher education, leads to processes that support Pierre Bourdieu's claims that higher education systems exist to perpetuate and replicate existing social, economic, and cultural divisions within society and Samuel Bowles and Herbert Gintis's Marxist claim that education is used by the elite classes to control the lower classes.[19]

Intentionally or not, selective admissions policies that prioritize criteria such as standardized test scores, high school curricular rigor and performance, and extracurricular and athletic participation favor students from higher socioeconomic backgrounds and disadvantage nonwhite students.[20] Reliance on cultural capital as a signal of merit compounds throughout a student's education, representing an educational version of the Matthew effect, in which a student's early access to cultural capital results in regular and consistent access to elite opportunities throughout their educational career and, ultimately, increases the likelihood of admission to an elite undergraduate institution.[21] Conversely, students from less privileged educational backgrounds are denied opportunities, creating a gap in the experiences valued by higher education. This gap becomes increasingly hard to overcome as they progress through their education.[22]

Fellowships sit at the peak of the Matthew effect, and many of the meritocracy-driven outcomes and processes have been reproduced within the field. Fellowships often have criteria such as academic engagement, creativity, leadership, and ambassadorial potential, and many of them share similar missions of cultivating a community of future world leaders to address global issues.[23] As in selective undergraduate admissions, fellowships typically have a large pool of highly qualified candidates and the subsequent need for evaluative processes that can identify promise and potential.[24] Accordingly, many fellowships have adopted holistic review processes analogous to those used by elite institutions, using essays, letters of recommendation, research activity, and extracurricular engagement as ways to evaluate an applicant's potential.[25] As in undergraduate admissions, critiques of these processes affirm that individual merit is being conflated with access to cultural capital, thereby reinforcing existing pathways to elite opportunity rather than expanding access to them.

As a response to these critiques, a new model of meritocracy has been proposed that Vikki Boliver and colleagues refer to as the meritocratic equity of opportunity model.[26] This model claims that equitable selection processes require accounting for the socioeconomic and demographic backgrounds of applicants, particularly as they relate to access to previous academic opportunity. A key initial step in doing so involves examining existing processes to identify where inequitable criteria—or attempts to evaluate those criteria—exist.

Within the field of fellowships, advisors can aid the shift toward more equitable meritocratic practices by incorporating explicitly antiracist strategies. We can play a role in nominating a diverse slate of candidates and actively supporting diverse voices and narratives in these processes. While gatekeeping is inherent in processes that require institutional nomination or endorsement, we can ensure that we are promoting awards to a diverse range of potential applicants and that we are highlighting narratives that broaden the image of who can be successful in these awards.

Attracting a demographically diverse range of applicants alone is insufficient to combat systemic racism. We must also examine how we work with students at every stage of the process, from interrogating cultural norms around writing to embracing different manifestations of leadership to cultivating applicants' agency by decentering ourselves as the bearers of knowledge.

Regarding writing pedagogy itself, a burgeoning movement exists to combat structural racism as it manifests in concepts of "standard" writing. Scholars such as Asao B. Inoue, Frankie Condon, and Vershawn Ashanti Young have demonstrated how the "norms" of academic and "professional" writing embody white supremacist ideologies, prioritizing the historical style and structure of educated white people in modern writing standards.[27] This standard contributes to a "double consciousness" on the part of students whose mother dialect varies from the accepted norms, whether because of linguistic practices rooted in race, culture, class, or region—and for nonnative English speakers.[28]

Additionally, this biased perception of "acceptable" writing can often lead to students of color, nonnative English speakers, poor and rural students, and many other marginalized groups being negatively evaluated against standards that are rooted in Whiteness.[29] In recent years, a growing number of scholars have called for writing instructors and evaluators to embrace students' natural dialects and writing styles instead of reinforcing these norms.

Antiracist Writing Workshop

In 2019, when I became the director of global awards at NYU, I was faced with supporting a much larger number of applicants to the most well-known postgraduate awards (e.g., Marshall, Mitchell, and Rhodes) than I had at previous institutions. That summer, I launched a cohort-based program called the Application Development Cohort (ADC) to support these applicants. Truth be told, it was initially a time-management strategy, an attempt to have one conversation with twenty students at a time rather than having the same basic conversation twenty times.

I quickly witnessed a number of additional benefits of the cohort model. Participants became engaged with each other's narratives and were eager to share with and learn from each other's experiences. After countless instances in which a participant made a point or introduced an idea that I had been preparing to say, I began to realize that I had been ignoring crucial collaborators in the fellowships advising process—the applicants themselves. What had once been a highly individualized and potentially isolating process had evolved into a community of knowledge sharing and communal support.

Seeking to find ways both to foster increased collaboration and to incorporate explicitly antiracist practices into my advising, I ultimately came upon *The Anti-racist Writing Workshop*, a 2021 memoir cum pedagogical guide for creative writing.[30] In the book, Felicia Rose Chavez details her experiences as a Chicana student navigating higher education, with a particular focus on the oppressive nature of the creative writing courses she took as both an undergraduate and graduate student. She offers an alternative model for writing instruction: one that acknowledges and flattens power, promotes authorial agency, and embraces multiple styles and voices.

While reading the text, I reflected on how I had been working with students on their writing. My primary method of providing feedback involved applicants sending me their essays, and me giving written feedback and editorial guidance. Even within early iterations of the cohort, writing feedback was primarily transactional and centered me as the expert on what a good essay *should* look like. My feedback was mainly filtered through the lens of attempting to guide students toward writing essays that would meet the expectations of an invisible or unknown panel of readers.

My advising process began to change after reading Chavez's text, which provides specific and actionable steps that writing instructors can take to dismantle legacies of white supremacy and structural racism within writing pedagogy. Three key features are representation, cocreation of central concepts, and author-driven workshop sessions. Each of these features is designed to cultivate feelings of inclusion and support for authors and to center authorial agency in the writing process. Beginning with the 2021 ADC, I have striven to incorporate elements of Chavez's approach into my pedagogy.

I have begun by focusing on representation and inclusion within the cohort program. I have sought to recruit a diverse cohort of students, representing a wide range of races and ethnicities, genders and sexual orientations, abilities, socioeconomic backgrounds, disciplines, and more. To do so, I have ensured that my outreach materials have featured both images and testimonials from a representative cross section of previous participants. I have also sought to ensure that alumni panels are similarly representative—and that they include participants who have achieved all levels of success with fellowships, including recipients, finalists, and applicants who did not advance beyond the preliminary stage.

When providing previous essays for participants to analyze and explore, I intentionally select writing that represents a wide range of demographics and lived experiences. Further, I seek to include a wide range of writing types and voices, demonstrating that successful essays need not align with perceived expectations concerning genre and style. When possible, I invite previous applicants to visit the cohort, providing insight into their writing style and approach and discussing how their essays evolved throughout the process. Additionally, I include both early and final drafts among the examples that I share, helping students see the evolution of an individual author's narrative throughout the writing process.

To help applicants develop their own understanding of award criteria, I facilitate discussions about the many criteria that these awards share. For example, rather than presenting a prescriptive definition of leadership, I encourage participants to share their perceptions of leadership, thereby providing examples that demonstrate the value and effectiveness of a wide range of leadership styles. We conduct similar exercises around ideas of mission and vision, ambassadorship, and academic excellence. Encouraging participants to cultivate their own conceptions of these criteria serves to decenter me as the singular authority on awards, instead helping participants better see themselves and their accomplishments as worthy of recognition.

This decentering of the fellowships advisor as the expert manifests throughout the process. We spend a part of one session discussing the legacies of these awards, highlighting their connection to historical oppressive practices (e.g., Cecil Rhodes's relationship to exploitative mining practices in sub-Saharan Africa and his explicitly racist and sexist outlooks; George Marshall's connection to World War II; the practices of billionaires such as Phil Knight and Stephen Schwarzman that enabled them to amass the wealth that endows these awards) and to current oppressive practices (e.g., elite higher education's connections to capitalism; the racist histories of selective admissions practices; the perception that applicants must exploit their personal trauma to succeed in awards). My intention is not to steer the applicants in any particular direction but to encourage them to make the choices that are right for them, thereby fostering a stronger sense of agency throughout the application process. I have had students come to a wide range of decisions regarding individual awards, from choosing not to apply to them to explicitly addressing their legacies in their application materials or to choosing to apply as a way to attempt to rewrite and reclaim these legacies. I firmly believe that there is no universal right choice for an applicant but that whatever informed choice they make is the right one for them.

This concept of agency sits at the core of the most revolutionary component of Chavez's pedagogy: the author-guided peer review process. In her book, Chavez discusses how the traditional method for creative writing workshops silences the author, requiring them to passively absorb critiques from fellow students. This approach is particularly deleterious for authors with marginalized identities, as it prioritizes the perspectives of the authors' peers, who often do not share those identities and therefore lack the cultural or lived experiences that inform the authors' writing. This approach can lead to feedback that either results in authors being forced to defend or explain perspectives that defy their peers' expectations or misses the point entirely.

I began modeling the ADC's feedback sessions around Chavez's suggestions and integrated a peer workshop stage after several weeks of guided discussion, facilitation, and writing exercises. During these workshops, each participant presents a piece of writing from their application to the group, with a set time for reading and feedback (typically twenty to twenty-five minutes). Before they read the piece, they present three to four framing questions that help their peers provide relevant feedback. These open-ended questions are designed to elicit specific and targeted input that actually serves the author's needs. They may ask such questions as, "Which anecdotes kept your attention the best?"; "When did you find your attention drifting?"; "How effectively did you find the two central themes interacting with each other?"; or "Where did you find yourself wanting more specific examples?" I ask the authors to send me their questions in advance so that I can help ensure that they have designed them to be open-ended and generative.

After reading the sample aloud, the author facilitates the feedback session. All participants must ask permission to share input, particularly if that input focuses on topics outside the author's framing questions. It is entirely up to the author to determine which feedback they would like to hear. For example, if a peer says, "I know you were looking for feedback on your conclusion, but I'd like to discuss the narrative about your mother," it is completely within the author's discretion to say no. While I have found that it is fairly unusual for an author to decline feedback from any of their peers, placing the power of the workshop squarely in the hands of the author has had a revolutionary effect on the subsequent conversations. I have observed that peers are thoughtful and direct when providing input, and authors become even more open to constructive suggestions.

Throughout the workshop sessions, I position myself as simply one of the group. I tend to withhold my feedback until later in the session and regularly find that the students make the same points that I would have made (and often even better and more succinctly). Admittedly, withholding my own feedback was one of the more challenging parts of the process for me. But while I enjoy giving constructive feedback to my students, embracing a process that attempts to subvert traditional power dynamics and center the needs of the author has both been an ego check for me and bolstered my confidence in the participants' ability to provide strong feedback.

Participants' reactions were immediate, strong, and positive. In postcohort assessment surveys, students shared the following perspectives:

> I enjoyed the writing workshops because they forced me to switch from writing drafts mostly for myself to thinking more deeply about how my work would be read by others, which was a push that I needed. I came away from the workshop with more insight and awareness of what I was trying to say and more options for how to structure and communicate that message.

> The level of personal attention and creation of a shared collaborative language in the actual workshops was unlike any process I've worked on. Writing the Essay or even my workshopping poetry course did not have the kind of weekly connection that the cohort found.

> The word that comes to mind with this process is "safety." More than any other writing development workshop or process, I felt able to share my work, be vulnerable, and accept feedback without fear of hurt or misunderstanding. I believe other workshops have been more helpful in refining my actual writing style and language, but this workshop was very well suited to refining my mission, vision, and story.

> The best part was the critiques—always constructive, really energized me in terms of figuring out new approaches to get my message across. Workshopping others' work was also super constructive and continually gave me ideas on how to improve my own application.[31]

Conclusion

While adapting Chavez's antiracist writing workshop techniques to my fellowships advising process is just one step toward more comprehensive antiracist fellowships practice, it has proved to be effective and inspirational. As a result of ongoing efforts to address structural racism and white supremacy in my fellowships practice, I have become a better advisor, learning to embrace a more diverse set of perspectives and voices and becoming more comfortable decentering myself as the ultimate expert for my students. I hope that this essay can serve as a starting point for anyone working within the field of fellowships to examine their own practices and incorporate approaches that create more inclusive and equitable environments for all potential fellowships applicants.

Notes

1. Alice Stone Ilchman, Warren F. Ilchman, and Mary Hale Tolar, "Strengthening Nationally and Internationally Competitive Scholarships: An Overview," in *The Lucky Few and the Worthy Many: Scholarship Competitions and the World's Future Leaders*, ed. Alice Stone Ilchman, Warren F. Ilchman, and Mary Hale Tolar (Bloomington: Indiana University Press, 2004), 1–31.
2. "Outreach and Diversity," Association of Marshall Scholars, https://marshallscholars.org/diversity.
3. "#BlackLivesMatter, Racism and Legacy: Reflections on the Past, Present, and Future of Rhodes Scholarships," Rhodes Trust, https://www.rhodeshouse.ox.ac.uk/impact-legacy/blacklivesmatter-racism-and-legacy/ (this URL is no longer available).
4. Elliot Gerson, letter to the editor, *American Oxonian*, Spring 2022, 17.
5. George J. Sefa Dei, "Critical Perspectives in Antiracism: An Introduction," *Canadian Review of Sociology/Revue Canadienne de Sociologie* 33, no. 3 (1996): 247–67.
6. H. Richard Milner, "Critical Race Theory and Interest Convergence as Analytic Tools in Teacher Education Policies and Practices," *Journal of Teacher Education* 54, no. 4 (2008): 332–46.
7. Christine Sleeter, "How White Teachers Construct Race," in *Race, Identity, and Representation in Education*, ed. Cameron McCarthy and Warren Crichlow (New York: Routledge Books, 1993), 157–72;

Janet E. Helms, *A Race Is a Nice Thing to Have: A Guide to Being a White Person or Understanding the White Persons in Your Life* (Hanover, NH: Microtraining Associates, 2008); Mary E. Earick, *Racially Equitable Teaching: Beyond the Whiteness of Professional Development for Early Childhood Educators (Rethinking Childhood)* (New York: Peter Lang, 2008); Laura Smith et al., "White Professors Teaching about Racism: Challenges and Rewards," *Counseling Psychologist* 45, no. 5 (2017): 651–68.

8. Nado Aveling, "Critical Whiteness Studies and the Challenges of Learning to Be a 'White Ally,'" *Borderlands* 3, no. 2 (2004): 1–10; Ellen M. Broido, "The Development of Social Justice Allies during College: A Phenomenological Investigation," *Journal of College Student Development* 41, no. 1 (2000): 3–18; Keith E. Edwards, "Aspiring Social Justice Ally Identity Development: A Conceptual Model," *NASPA Journal* 43, no. 4 (2006): 39–60.

9. Gloria S. Boutte and Tambra O. Jackson, "Advice to White Allies: Insights from Faculty of Color," *Race, Ethnicity and Education* 17, no. 5 (2014): 623–42.

10. Derek W. Sue et al., "Racial Microaggressions and Difficult Dialogues on Race in the Classroom," *Cultural Diversity and Ethnic Minority Pedagogy* 15, no. 2 (2009): 183–90; Robin DiAngelo, *White Fragility: Why It's So Hard for White People to Talk about Racism* (Boston: Beacon, 2018).

11. Teresa J. Guess, "The Social Construction of Whiteness: Racism by Intent, Racism by Consequence," *Critical Sociology* 32, no. 4 (2006): 649–73.

12. Jahneille Cunningham, "Missing the Mark: Standardized Testing as Epistemological Erasure in U.S. Schooling," *Power and Education* 11, no. 1 (2020): 111–20; Diane Lynn Gusa, "White Institutional Presence: The Impact of Whiteness on Campus Climate," *Harvard Educational Review* 80, no. 4 (2010): 464–89; Richard R. Valencia, *Dismantling Contemporary Deficit Thinking: Educational Thought and Practice* (New York: Routledge Books, 2010).

13. Zeus Leonardo, "The Souls of White Folk: Critical Pedagogy, Whiteness Studies, and Globalization Discourse," *Race, Ethnicity, and Education* 5, no. 1 (2002): 29–50; Owen J. Dwyer and John Paul Jones, "White Socio-spatial Epistemology," *Social and Cultural Geography* 1, no. 2 (2000): 209–19; Ellen Swartz, "Diversity: Gatekeeping Knowledge and Maintaining Inequalities," *Review of Educational Research* 79, no. 2 (2009): 1044–83.

14. Gusa, "White Institutional Presence."

15. Michael D. Young, *The Rise of the Meritocracy* (New York: Routledge Books, 1958).

16. Martin A. Trow, "The Expansion and Transformation of Higher Education," *International Review of Education* 18, no. 1 (1972): 61–84; Anna M. Zimdars, *Meritocracy and the University: Selective Admissions in England and the United States* (London: Bloomsbury Academic, 2016).

17. Daniel Markovits, *The Meritocracy Trap: How America's Foundational Myth Feeds Inequality, Dismantles the Middle Class, and Devours the Elite* (New York: Penguin, 2019).

18. Pierre Bourdieu, "The Forms of Capital," in *Handbook of Theory and Research for the Sociology of Education*, ed. John G. Richardson (Westport, CT: Greenwood, 1986), 241–58; Pierre Bourdieu and Jean-Claude Passerson, *Reproduction in Education, Society, and Culture* (London: Sage, 1977).

19. Pierre Bourdieu, "Systems of Education and Systems of Thought," in *Knowledge and Control: New Directions in the Sociology of Education*, ed. Michael F. D. Young (London: Collier-Macmillan, 1971), 338–58; Samuel Bowles and Herbert Gintis, *Schooling in Capitalist America: Educational Reform and the Contradictions of Economic Life* (New York: Basic Books, 1976).

20. James Crouse and Dale Trusheim, *The Case against the SAT* (Chicago: University of Chicago Press, 1988); Christopher Jencks and Meredith Phillips, "The Black-White Test Score Gap: An Introduction," in *The Black-White Test Score Gap*, ed. Christopher Jencks and Meredith Phillips (Washington, DC: Brookings Institution Press, 1998), 1–51; Michael N. Bastedo, Joseph E. Howard, and Allyson Flaster, "Holistic Admissions after Affirmative Action. Does 'Maximizing' the High School Curriculum Matter?," *Educational Evaluation and Policy Analysis* 38, no. 2 (2016): 389–409; Jay Gabler and Jason Kaufman, "Chess, Cheerleading, Chopin: What Gets You into College?," *Contexts* 5, no. 2 (2006): 45–49; Jason Kaufman and Jay Gabler, "Cultural Capital and the Extracurricular Activities of Girls and Boys in the College Attainment Process," *Poetics* 32, no. 2 (2004): 145–68.

21. Robert K. Merton, "The Matthew Effect in Science: The Reward and Communication Systems of Science Are Considered," *Science* 159 (1968): 56–63; Markovits, *Meritocracy Trap*.

22. Alan Kerckhoff and Elizabeth J. Glennie, "The Matthew Effect in American Education," *Research in Sociology of Education and Socialization* 12 (1999): 35–66.

23. Ilchman, Ilchman, and Tolar, "Strengthening."

24. Stanley J. Heginbotham, "Art and Science in Strengthening Scholarship Selection," in Ilchman, Ilchman, and Tolar, *Lucky Few and the Worthy Many*, 62–103.

25. Ilchman, Ilchman, and Tolar, "Strengthening."

26. Vikki Boliver et al., "Reconceptualizing Fair Access to Highly Selective Universities," *Higher Education* 84 (2002): 85–100.

27. Asao B. Inoue, *Antiracist Writing Assessment Ecologies: Teaching and Assessing Writing for a Socially Just Future* (Anderson, SC: Parlor, 2015); Frankie Condon, "Beyond the Known: Writing Centers and the Work of Anti-racism," *Writing Center Journal* 27, no. 2 (2007): 19–38; Vershawn A. Young, "'Nah, We Straight': An Argument against Code Switching," *JAC* 29, no. 1–2 (2009): 49–76.

28. Young, "'Nah, We Straight.'"

29. James A. Baldwin, "African-American and European-American Cultural Differences as Assessed by the Worldview Paradigm: An Empirical Analysis," *Western Journal of Black Studies* 14, no. 1 (1990): 38–52; Clevis Headley, "Delegitimizing the Normativity of 'Whiteness': A Critical Africana Philosophical Study of the Metaphoricity of 'Whiteness,'" in *What White Looks Like*, ed. George Yancy (New York: Routledge, 2004), 87–106; Ross Chambers, "The Unexamined," in *Whiteness: A Critical Reader*, ed. Mike Hill (New York: New York University Press, 1997), 187–203.

30. Felicia Rose Chavez, *The Anti-racist Writing Workshop: How to Decolonize the Creative Classroom* (Chicago: Haymarket Books, 2021).

31. Kurt Davies, "ADC Mini Assessment Responses" (unpublished manuscript 2022).

PART III

Developing the Profession

8

Zero Searches Found. Try Again?

The Journey of a Fellowships Research Collective

CATHERINE SALGADO

n the summer of 2020, Lauren Tuckley of Georgetown University sent an email to me at Arizona State University, Jessie McCrary (Emory University), and Elise Rudt (University of Notre Dame). "I'm writing to see if there is appetite among this group," she began, "to get together to discuss possible collaborative research." Although none of us had ever met each other in person, as graduate students who were also full-time fellowships advisors, we had shared some camaraderie (and commiseration). "I think there is ample opportunity at our professional and academic nexus that's well worth exploring," Tuckley continued. As the responses came in, I began to realize a shared mutual interest in finding ways to incorporate fellowships into our academic research, as well as a general desire to improve the transparency of fellowships processes as a whole.

Little did we know that Tuckley's email would initiate a research project that would span three years and lead us to form the FRC, or Fellowships Research Collective. I will admit, had I known our research project would take that long, I might have been more hesitant to begin. But I am glad that I joined that first Zoom meeting, as the work has been beneficial in professional, scholarly, and personal ways far beyond what any of us imagined. What began as the pursuit of acceptance into the scholarly world by four hopeful graduate students became a much larger negotiation of our scholarly identities. Starting and continuing this research collaborative meant we had a shared space to negotiate, discuss, and process our overlapping work as fellowships advisors and emerging scholars as we grew into and beyond those spaces. In the National Association of Fellowships Advisors' spirit of transparency, vulnerability, and growth, this scholarly collaborative work has resulted in far more than we anticipated.

When Tuckley first reached out to us about forming a research group, the waves of the pandemic, Black Lives Matter movement, and ensuing advocacy movements around housing, health care, and debt, to name a few, were swirling around us. Within the fellowships world, most programs had been canceled by the summer of 2020. "Recruitment" for any program at that time felt pointless, especially when many of our students had been forced to prematurely end their grants abroad and needed immediate attention and aid. We were reacting and responding to a seemingly never-ending series of crises in real time, with little guarantee that things really would get better—quite the departure from our pre-pandemic lives. As with a controlled burn during an Arizona spring, we were used to predicting when and where certain fires would be based on the familiar rhythms of each application cycle. Instead, there was just fire everywhere, and no cycle to complete.

So I was relieved when what I thought would be a very serious initial conversation about methods and journals turned out to be nothing about research. Instead, we commiserated about the many challenges we were each facing. In addition to pandemic-related stressors, we felt collectively suspended between graduate work and work-work, and we were exhausted from toggling between the two. In the eyes of the academy, we were "nontraditional" graduate students. When asked, *What do you do for a living?* there was always a "but" in our response. *I'm a scholarship advisor, but it's a different kind of scholarship. I'm a graduate student, but I'm part time. I'm a staff member, but I also teach.* When McCrary, Rudt, Tuckley, and I connected, we created a space to be all of these things at once without some lengthy explanation.

After our initial meeting, we continued our conversation informally throughout the summer of 2020 over Zoom and WhatsApp. We took inventory of the kinds of patterns and challenges we faced in our respective roles, such as application barriers (both hidden and explicit), feedback and revision processes, and competing stake-holder needs. We pointed out the discomfort of training intellectu-ally in one area of the academy but gathering professional expertise in another, and we laid out our altruistic and practical motivations for pursuing fellowships-related research. In essence, we wanted to expand fellowships advice and best practices beyond anecdotal evi-dence while simultaneously streamlining our graduate workload. But we felt a tension between our commitment made as National Association of Fellowships Advisors members to value process over the product, and the graduate school pressures to produce scholar-ship and develop our own scholarly status. We wanted to convince others in our field that fellowships mattered and had a place in schol-arly research, but we felt we lacked the professional capital to back up that claim.

The pandemic brought on a number of challenges, but it also invited us to reflect on our lives and to consider what we would do differently if given the chance. So we asked ourselves, what would our worlds look like if we combined the hemispheres of our intellectual and professional lives? This question would eventually become the shared purpose of our group. Two months of informal brainstorming eventually led to a call to action from Tuckley, in an email that very well could have had the subject line, "So are we doing this research thing or what?"

In her email, she identified five "next steps" to begin our collabora-tive project:

- Identify research on writing prompts across disciplines.
- Identify "touchstone" articles, or formative contributions that are commonly referenced.
- Keep an eye out for journals that might be a good home for this kind of research.
- Develop working research questions.
- Explore alternative ideas, since there was nothing formal com-mitting us to the topic at hand.

Fellowships advisors come from a variety of academic disciplines and experiences, which is exactly what makes our professional association rich in its perspectives and knowledge building. But that breadth would also be a major point of tension as we worked toward selecting a topic and research method. Despite each of us being loosely affiliated with "writing studies," bringing our four fields—composition, linguistics, technical communication, and rhetoric—together would prove to be more difficult than we imagined.

Our first task was to complete the "journal sweep" to better understand audience needs, identify journal patterns, and collectively harness our expertise. As we searched, we took into account preferences for specific methodologies, representation of single-author versus coauthored papers, populations (first-year students, graduate students, multilingual learners, etc.), focus (e.g., pedagogy, theory), and special editions. We considered all of the key journals in writing studies, including *Writing across the Curriculum, English for Specific Purposes, Written Communication,* and the *Journal of Technical Writing and Communication,* to name a few.

But flipping through archives of online journal issues felt a lot like reading through examples of personal statements in the hopes of finding one that "sounds" like you. Ctrl+F "fellowship personal statements." Ctrl+F "endorsements." Ctrl+F "competitive scholarships."

Zero searches found. Try again?

Bathed in a glow of blue light, I would retype an offering into my all-knowing Google Scholar search box, only for it to throw me a thesis from 1998 and shrug its shoulders. Discouraged, confused, and slightly disheartened, we responded to the repeated dead ends as any graduate student would: with a shared Google folder and dozens of spreadsheets. What we lacked in research method expertise we made up for with enthusiasm and unusually developed organizational skills honed by years of fellowships advising.

Our uncertainty about whether fellowships could realistically fit within a particular academic discourse grew. Although fellowships advising was firmly embedded in the academic ecosystem, the writing that we interacted with as advisors did not fit into the boxes provided by many of the writing-focused journals, most of which gave preference to first-year writing and classroom-based or field-specific writing instruction (e.g., writing for engineers). Fellowships-related writing was both applied and iterative, it was process oriented, and it operated within a complex chain of behind-the-scenes selection systems. Explaining the differences in scope and size of various fellowships offices or programs to a lay audience is laborious and difficult, particularly since some operate within and alongside honors colleges, study abroad offices, writing centers, or career services offices. Add to that the task of explaining the inner workings of an internal nomination process, the various hats fellowships advisors often wear (e.g., academic advisors, faculty, or administrators), and context for our research seemed impossible.

The aspects of fellowships that make it such a complex and rich site of inquiry were exactly what was complicating our research design. Looking back on this moment in the literature review process, it is clear to me now that we were asking all the wrong questions. We were approaching the journals with the mentality of, "What do they want to hear?" when we should have been asking, "What do we have to say?" So we switched tracks: rather than aligning our study with the preferences of a single journal, we pursued answers to these questions instead:

1. What kind of data are available to us? How can we use this to improve existing processes while also adhering to institutional review board (IRB) standards?
2. Can these data be reconciled across four institutional settings, given our differences in size, resources, and internal protocols?
3. What qualitative or quantitative method could all four of us realistically implement, given our academic training in disparate fields?

Even given these parameters, the amount of data and the means by which we could analyze it was overwhelming. It would be another two months before we settled on a research design. Upon the closure of another Fulbright cycle in 2020, I sent an email with the innocuous subject line, "Before the thought escapes me." In it, I suggested that we conduct a rhetorical moves analysis of letters of recommendation (LORs), similar to the research conducted by Matt Kessler on personal statements.[1] I proposed that we consider letters written for applications to the Fulbright ETA, Goldwater, or Truman.

LORs had been on my mind for a while. During the inception of our research group, I was completing a master's thesis in linguistics that aimed to unite textual analysis research methods with fellowships by evaluating stance markers in Goldwater recommendation letters. I was particularly interested in stance markers called *hedges* and *boosters*, which allow writers to convey their personal attitudes, judgments, or assessment. Hedges, which include terms like *maybe*, *perhaps*, and *possibly*, allow writers to show doubt, express an opinion, and convey humility and respect, whereas boosters, such as *always*, *clearly*, and *certainly*, are considered intensifying features that enable writers to build in-group membership, restrict negotiating space, and display commitment to their claim.[2] Within the field of linguistics, hedges and boosters have been a steady topic of interest, with studies exploring their use across written and spoken mediums, across genders, and in specific speech acts. I hypothesized that writers would be more likely to use boosters in their recommendations of a candidate to support their claims about the candidate's suitability for an award.

The findings proved otherwise. To my surprise, writers in the sample of fifty-one letters employed a high frequency (59 percent) of hedges in their recommendations. When I looked closely at the hedging terms in context, however, it became clear that writers hedged in positive ways (e.g., "He is quite *possibly the best* student I have ever taught"; "I have *no doubt* she will succeed"). Had I not considered context, I might have drawn incomplete conclusions about the writers in my sample and their community, such as that STEM recommenders are less likely to "boost" their candidates. It was then that my question changed from, "To what frequency do STEM recommenders use hedges and boosters?" to, "How do the discrete hedging and boosting terms function persuasively?"

I have never been more grateful for a failed hypothesis, for it sparked discussion for our October meeting and would lead us to our eventual study. While discussing the contextual limitations of "bottom-up" approaches such as text mining for discrete terms,

Tuckley pointed out socio-rhetorical analysis as a potential solution. In its essence, socio-rhetorical analysis combines analysis of the social environment with rhetorical analysis, to consider the context in which texts are conceived. While it is important to note what a text says, a socio-rhetorical lens also wants to know the ways in which a text functions in relation to the social systems in which it operates. This method would allow us to not only analyze what a text says but also draw on our expertise as members of the social community from which the text is generated and used for interpretation.

We considered what kinds of fellowship texts would be best suited for socio-rhetorical methods, such as personal statements, endorsement letters, and statements of purpose. We eventually decided to pursue LORs as an official study for a few reasons: the scope of the project would allow each of us to draw on our professional expertise; we could each contribute data in a standardized way; we all felt a need for data-driven advice for LOR writing; and LORs as a textual subject were relevant to a variety of academic fields. We collectively read hundreds of LORs each year as part of our job duties, and we wanted to draw on our insider knowledge as fellowships advisors in a way that added depth to our overall discussion of how LORs reach their exigence. We chose to analyze LORs written for the Truman Scholarship, largely because that program's data were available to all four of us across multiple application cycles.

The next ten months would be spent completing IRB approval, creating our coding scheme, testing and refining it, and drafting a manuscript. We decided to swing big and submitted to a high-impact journal on our first go. We received this response:

> Thank you for your patience while I waited for the reviews of your manuscript. I have considered your manuscript and our reviewers' comments and recommendations at length and, unfortunately, I have decided not to publish your work.
>
> In the hopes of assisting you as you revise this work for another journal, I have included the reviewers' comments below. While Reviewer 1 suggests you revise part of this work for publication in a non-academic journal, I believe this work may well find a place in *Composition*

Forum, Journal of Business and Technical Communication, or *English for Specific Purposes.*

As we read through the reviewer comments, our group chat lit up like Times Square. The editorial board had raised a number of questions and concerns, but the most surprising one was anonymous reviewer 2's suggestion that we had obtained our sample of letters illegitimately, despite our study being IRB approved. We sensed an underlying tone of disbelief from reviewers, as if we had somehow intercepted these letters as they traveled between writer and foundation. We felt misunderstood (*do they know that we are working professionals AND graduate students?*), undervalued (*do they understand the depth of our sample?*), and a little embarrassed. We thought we had been clear about the nature of our work, but we had failed, rhetorically, to connect with our audience.

That first rejection was a much-needed wake-up call for all of us. We could not assume a sympathetic audience, and we needed to explain in greater detail why our offices would handle application materials on behalf of a foundation for internal nomination processes. Over the course of two separate revisions and resubmissions to different journals, we made the following key revisions to our design:

- Clarified the role of fellowships offices and the nomination process
- Sharpened the literature review to support specific claims rather than providing a summary of studies
- Explicated the need for LOR research that illuminates the constituent elements of an LOR (i.e., recurring rhetorical features) as well as how the LOR fulfills its persuasive purpose (i.e., situated interpretations of its discourse)
- Revisited our letter sample and narrowed our focus

The following is the result of that process. I will say that providing a "final study" feels a lot like providing a submitted personal statement draft for a workshop. It seems shiny and polished, but this project was anything but straightforward. With that caveat in mind, what follows is a synopsis of our submitted study, which has since been offered conditional acceptance into the writing studies journal *Written Communication.*

Titled "Situating Evaluation and Authority: Direct Sponsorship in Letters of Recommendation," our final study analyzed eighty-four LORs submitted for Truman nomination across four institutions and four cycles. When we initially read through the entire collection of letters, we noticed that LORs from nonacademic writers (e.g., government, nonprofit, and private sectors) were markedly different from the LORs written by academic writers, with the most obvious difference being their length. On average, nonacademic writers wrote nearly half as much as academic writers. Therefore, we restricted the sample to academic writers, which we defined as those who work in student-facing roles at undergraduate institutions and facilitate students' academic growth and professionalization. This category includes faculty members, administrative directors, and cocurricular advisors. We noticed that academic writers were often writing across all three letter types for Truman (public service, leadership, and academic LORs), and we wanted to understand how academic writers might enact particular moves across LOR types.

Given our group's previous experience in socio-rhetorical analysis, as well as our collective familiarity with qualitative research methods, we decided to use a Swalesian move-step analysis. John Swales formalized the move-step method as a tool for language learners to better understand the form and functional organization of important documents in their target language.[3] Moves encapsulate the rhetorical purpose, intention, or theme of a series of sentences, while steps discuss the way that an author expresses that intention. For example, in a research article, one of the first "moves" would be to establish a problem, with the "step" referring to the act of identifying a gap in the literature. This approach allows us to identify recurring rhetorical moves in a way that is not limited to location, such as introduction, body, and conclusion frameworks, and also allows us to consider ways in which the expectations of the genre are carried out in letter writers' compositions.

The rhetorical moves occurring with the greatest frequency were (1) explaining applicant relationships, (2) expressing affective response, (3) discussing witnessed noncourse or nonresearch performance, (4) listing traits without evidence, (5) discussing unwitnessed accomplishments, (6) comparing applicants to others, and (7) offering an invitation to contact.

One of the most interesting patterns we noticed in our sample concerned the ways in which academic writers positioned themselves in relation to the candidate as well as the reader. While LOR writers certainly made specific moves to endorse a candidate, such as explaining the nature of their professional relationship, these endorsements were often embedded within the writers' own establishment of credibility:

I have taught leadership courses at . . . [prominent institutions] for 16 years. Over that time, I have had the pleasure of getting to know over 500 undergraduate students. [This student] ranks among the best of all the students that completed my class.

In two decades as a professor, during which I have endorsed several candidates eventually selected for Truman, Rhodes, and Marshall scholarships, I consider [student] among the top set. . . . Having benefited myself from study at Oxford University on a [prestigious] scholarship, I am sure [student] would thrive in and greatly contribute to the Truman Scholarship community, and any university in which he studies.

As we can see in both excerpts, the writers establish their credibility in a number of ways, such as highlighting their number of years in academia, the institutions at which they have taught, the number of students they have mentored, and even their affiliation with particular grants and institutions. The recurring pattern of credentialing stirred a larger conversation on the ways in which academic writers commodified their credibility on behalf of applicants.

This realization led us to propose "direct sponsorship" as a theoretical concept with explanatory power. Drawing inspiration from Deborah Brandt's concept of literacy sponsorship, we considered the ways in which writers mediate access to knowledge and scarce opportunities outside informal literacy contexts.[4] We saw direct sponsorship as explicit advocacy conducted on behalf of an individual who requests access to a closed community. In other words, direct sponsorship is a means by which recommenders use their own expertise and social or professional capital to vouch for candidates. The justification presented by the writer is persuasive only so far as the selection committee considers the recommender a legitimate authority in relation to the opportunity's selection objectives. This legitimacy is primarily derived from the recommender's ability to relate and connect to the community for which the applicant seeks access.

This desire to legitimize aspects of our professional and personal identities was a feeling we knew all too well. Even with our best attempts to employ a process-oriented growth mindset in our graduate work, we could not help but feel defensive over our status as nontraditional graduate students. The doubt cast from anonymous reviewer 2 in our initial journal rejection was proof that our identities as graduate students could, and would, be met with suspicion and undermine our credibility as scholars. As we discussed our findings, we were quick to point out that, if asked to write a LOR, we would likely highlight our professional titles as staff over our titles as PhD students. We were particularly sensitive to how our position as PhD students might lead us to be perceived as inexperienced by academic audiences, despite some of us being directors and upper-level managers of our individual fellowship units. It became clear that LORs were not solely "third-party" evaluations, as we implicitly believed, but rather sites of complex identity work that also operated as a form of academic currency.

The results of our study were illuminating from both a scholarly and personal perspective. Our findings invited us to reconsider which aspects of our identities we privilege in certain professional contexts, and which ones we would be most likely to call on to endorse one another. Furthermore, it allowed us to confront aspects of ourselves we were most likely to downplay for fear of losing perceived authority. But this underlying fear—this need to hide aspects of ourselves in an attempt to gain and retain scholarly status—was exactly what bell hooks describes as *compartmentalization*, a defining characteristic of patriarchal structures.[5] For us as women research-ers, compartmentalization meant alternating between domestic and emotional roles as caretakers or spouses in our personal lives while also pursuing the individual achievement, academic rank, and hier-archical prestige so valued by the scholarly world, where the former roles were often seen as, at best, distractions or, at worst, liabilities. The chaos of the COVID-19 pandemic had already weakened the walls that separated our own compartments, and our newfound understanding of identity performance in the academic world broke the dam. We no longer felt obligated to keep the disparate aspects of our identities separate and distinct.

One particular Zoom meeting comes to mind. Tuckley is onscreen, and the door behind her swings open as her daughter shuffles into the frame. Her daughter stops and holds a blanket up to her face, mumbling. Tuckley turns around to respond as we all, in our separate tiny thumbnails, smile and wave. Suddenly, the tiny floating head dis-appears below the camera line. Tuckley punches the mute button a moment too late, and the sound of retching reaches our earphones as her daughter throws up all over the floor. We let out a collective, "Ohhhhh nooo," and laugh. Unmute. "Yeah, guys . . . I gotta go." End meeting for all? Her daughter is fine and recovers from the stomach bug twenty-four hours later. Life goes on, the research continues.

If we had remained committed to compartmentalization, we might have stopped at our first journal rejection. I would have never seen Rudt's giant Maine Coon cat or learned that McCrary is incredibly gifted at sewing and knitting. I would not have seen Tuckley handed, like a *Game of Thrones* character, an enormous sword upon passing her doctoral defense. (Yes, she really received a sword.) At times, the work was messy, but it also brought freedom and kindness and com-munity and all the things bell hooks refers to as "wholeness."

When I first conceived this chapter, my original intent was to share our group's research findings (and the struggle to produce and publish them) with a sympathetic audience. What I realized during the drafting and revision process, however, was that while we cer-tainly faced defeat and doubt in many forms, this piece is not really about the redemption arc of being rejected and trying again. Nor is it about "pushing through" the hard times of losing loved ones, transitioning out of graduate programs and into graduate programs, moving to new homes and new states, or writing through surgeries and various illnesses (all of which occurred over the course of our research project). These are simply facts of life; they are events that would have transpired regardless of whether we created a research group. The difference, I would argue, is the community of support we built despite the temptation to take the easier route to isolate and retreat. In a profession where one-person offices are the norm, isolation may feel more comfortable and familiar to us than we even realize. Undertaking a collaborative research project created new spaces in which we negotiated the pressures brought on by our overlapping identities and roles within the academy—many of which frequently competed with the National Association of Fellowships Advisors' spirit of transparency, vulnerability, and growth.

I do not want to understate the difficulty of sustaining such an intense project over the period of three years. I recognize that fellowships-related research is sparse because of our recent inception as a profession and site of scholarly inquiry. Rather, I hoped to provide a realistic snapshot of how our group came to be, how we harnessed our strengths and field-specific expertise, and the ways in which collaborative research groups can add to our lives beyond a line in our CV. I am eager for fellowships to be recognized in the field of writing studies, but I know that will come in time, and as a result, rather than a goal, of consistent collaboration across our institutions. As we reflect on our time spent together at various conferences and workshops, I wonder how we might view research not as academic currency, or a task to be completed, but rather as a long-term investment in the relationships that make the profession whole.

Notes

1. Matt Kessler, "A Text Analysis and Gatekeepers' Perspectives of a Promotional Genre: Understanding the Rhetoric of Fulbright Grant Statements," *English for Specific Purposes* 60 (October 2020): 182–92.
2. Ken Hyland, *Hedging in Scientific Research Articles* (Philadelphia: John Benjamins, 1998).

3. John M. Swales, *Research Genres: Explorations and Applications* (New York: Cambridge University Press, 2004).
4. Deborah Brandt, *Literacy in American Lives* (New York: Cambridge University Press, 2001).
5. bell hooks, *The Will to Change: Men, Masculinity, and Love* (New York: Atria Books, 2004).

9

Beyond the Pandemic

Harnessing Insights from Bichronous Online
Teaching to Inform Fellowships Advising

RICHELLE BERNAZZOLI AND
MEREDITH RAUCHER SISSON

I n March 2020, as we were first beginning to understand the extent and impact of the COVID-19 pandemic, the fellowships advising community was gearing up for the launch of new application cycles for many of our most subscribed-to awards, including Fulbright. As institutions scrambled to move operations into the virtual space, we reimagined our fellowships advising process without many of the practices we had relied on up to that point, such as in-person informational sessions, class visits, and workshops. Fellowships advisors who also have teaching responsibilities were simultaneously working out the ideal balances of synchronous and asynchronous pedagogical approaches as we adapted our courses from in-person to online modalities, often with the help of dedicated experts in our institutions' centers for teaching and learning.

The authors of this essay each found that many of the best teaching practices we became acquainted with during that time allowed us to rethink fellowships advising approaches and learning outcomes for applicants in fruitful ways. Pedagogical methods that leverage a blend of synchronous and asynchronous engagement and emphasize active learning, such as team-based generative activities, often using digital tools, allowed us to improve our virtual advising dramatically. Of course, there had always been a need for advising practices that could engage students remotely, considering how much of our work on fall fellowships occurs over the summer, when many of our advisees are away from our campuses. But the massive shift to virtual education in those first months of the COVID-19 pandemic helped us formalize and systematize our approaches in ways that have permanently changed our fellowships advising for the better.

From Organization to Impact: Online Tools and Intentional Instructional Design

Our conversations with members of the fellowships advising community have made clear that the utilization of our institutions' learning management systems (LMSs), such as Blackboard and Canvas, has become, for many of us, a mainstay in how we recruit, track, and disseminate resources to fellowships advisees. But we want to emphasize in what follows that the shift necessitated by the pandemic illuminated that such tools are components of a broader pedagogical strategy, rather than constituting the strategy itself. In short, we were compelled to think about using online pedagogical tools in a richer way, rather than just using an LMS to organize static resources. This has involved conceptualizing the application cycle as a course with clear beginning and end points (i.e., the initial informational session and national deadline, respectively), and a lot of cohort-based and individuated engagement and progress in between.

Our intensified collaboration with the teaching centers on our campuses helped us to think more intentionally about learning outcomes *first* and then use backward design to envision the fellowships application cycle with a comprehensive framework. The learning outcomes we identified across the various fellowship application processes include but are not limited to award basics, leveraging networks, audience analysis, personal statement as genre, integrative learning (synthesizing knowledge and skills gained from disparate life experiences), proposal development, and collaborative and cohort-based learning.

With learning outcomes identified, we asked how we could create a cohesive learning experience for large cohorts of applicants who were scattered across geographic locations, time zones, and phases of life (some still students; some alumni). Much of the inspiration for this can be found in the literature on online education. A range of studies, many conducted in the wake of the mass transition to online teaching from March 2020 onward, demonstrated that a blend of synchronous and asynchronous technologies and instructional approaches can optimize online learning in contexts from K–12 to postsecondary education.[1] The term *bichronous design* refers to educational strategies that utilize both synchronous and asynchronous engagement of students.[2] Bichronous instructional design *intentionally* blends the synchronous and asynchronous, pairing real-time meetings, in which peer-to-peer active learning can take place, with activities that students can complete independently and on their own time. Modalities include asynchronous tools (email, announcements, discussion forums, quizzes, assignment submissions, recorded videos, peer review) and synchronous tools (instant messaging, collaborative tools such as interactive whiteboards, polling, video and audio conferencing, breakout room discussions in online platforms, peer review).[3]

Florence Martin, Drew Polly, and Albert Ritzhaupt highlight the benefits of bichronous design for learning cohorts in teacher education programs, nursing faculty training, and an MBA course—all instructional contexts where flexibility is a desirable characteristic.[4] Similarly, this approach best accommodates fellowships applicants, who are fitting this work in around full course schedules and sometimes full-time jobs, or who may be in different time zones as we work with them, particularly over the summer. The blend of modalities and content formats provides variety to suit different learning preferences, and also increases equity of access.

In traditional teaching contexts, bichronous design enhances learning outcomes, increases student persistence in a course, and improves student perceptions of a course.[5] However, in fellowships advising, student buy-in differs from that in courses. While many of us, as fellowships advisors, try to institute as many mechanisms as we can to motivate students to engage with the full scope of our offerings, we often do so with more *carrots* than *sticks*, and engagement over a semester's or summer's worth of application support programming can be inconsistent from one student to the next. Yet we have found that bichronous approaches are ideal for this scenario. As fellowships advisors, we are learning-outcome oriented, and we care very much about persistence—in the case of our work, this means follow-through on a particular fellowship application. Finally, we know that perception of the application process matters—the more explicit we are about learning outcomes, the more likely it is that students will walk away with a sense of growth and achievement, even if they do not receive a fellowship.

Self-directed learning (or taking responsibility for one's own learning outcomes) has also been highlighted as an important factor in successful online learning.[6] We argue that this is especially true in the case of fellowships advising, where students are not compelled to see the process through to completion in the same way they are for traditional courses that they are taking for grades and degree requirements. Hence, the well-constructed online learning resources for fellowships application processes must leverage the specific motivations of applicants to encourage self-directedness and inspire engagement with our materials.

Embracing Bichronicity: Two Cases

Richelle Bernazzoli, Carnegie Mellon University

The first information session our office held after Carnegie Mellon University went virtual in March 2020 was our annual Fulbright information session. What was once an in-person event was now held online, to overwhelmingly positive effect. In the past, we had relied on newly selected Fulbright grantees, or Fulbright alumni who happened to be on campus, to form an in-person panel of speakers. With the session held online, new possibilities opened up— the ETA alumnus who was working in international development in Washington, DC; the research grantee who was still carrying out their project abroad; the newly selected grantee who spoke excitedly about their project plans from their childhood bedroom. We had record attendance from students, alumni, faculty, and staff. We have not held an in-person Fulbright information session since.

This is not to downplay the value of in-person events, but that spring 2020 session alerted us to the possibility of engaging a wider audience that we could, but did not, leverage until the remote working conditions compelled us to do so. After that, more engagement opportunities took shape over the summer. One of the fellowship recruitment challenges on our campus is that the month of April quickly gets away from us. The Spring Carnival, a long-standing and cherished university tradition that includes several days off from classes for community celebration, amusement rides, alumni gatherings, and more, ensures that we have the campus community's attention for a brief window of time between mid-March and the end of the semester. I had long wanted to do more than just offer informational sessions, hoping to find the right timing for writing workshops and cohort building before students are consumed by finals, commencement, and the start of summer internships, research, and study abroad.

What resulted from that 2020 application cycle and remains in place now (with iterative refinements over time) is a recruitment and advising strategy that leans into bichronicity, rather than seeing the end of the semester as a time that we lose substantial engagement with our applicant cohorts. This was a fundamental shift from discrete recruitment events to continuous recruitment and retention of the cohort, providing multiple cohort touchpoints between the initial informational session and the campus deadline (Figure 9.1).

I had just had the experience of adapting my newly designed history course to be delivered virtually, with a mix of synchronous and asynchronous engagement (though I had not learned the term *bichronous* yet at that time), and I had worked with a teaching consultant in Carnegie Mellon's Eberly Center for Teaching and Learning Innovation to create active learning strategies that fostered peer-to-peer discussion and collaborative generation of content. In teaching that course in the new "pandemic normal" during spring 2020, I learned that we all quickly burn out listening to one person speak on Zoom for an extended period of time, and that breakout rooms quickly lose their utility if they are not employing well-structured prompts.

With these lessons in mind, I redesigned our Fulbright proposal and personal statement writing workshops, employing some of the

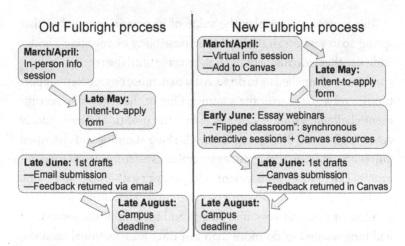

Figure 9.1. Comparing Carnegie Mellon University's old (pre–March 2020) and new (post–March 2020) Fulbright processes. From April to August, the new process seeks to foster continuous interaction as a cohort, hosting both static and interactive resources that can be engaged bichronously.

peer-supported and generative activities that had served me well in a traditional course. In order to support faculty as they adapted their courses for online, bichronous delivery, the Eberly Center compiled and promoted various ways to use digital tools to foster meaningful real-time engagement and make productive use of breakout-room discussions. One that I had utilized in my history course—Google Jamboard—seemed promising for a collaborative, generative exercise on developing Fulbright proposals. I devised a Jamboard activity for our synchronous online proposal writing workshops that distilled the components of the proposal into a four-part scheme: what/where/how/why for study and research proposals, and why/what/how/who for ETA proposals. I then created custom Jamboard frames with these schemes (Figure 9.2). In breakout rooms, participants took time to consider the schemes on their own and then discussed them as groups. They then used the sticky note feature in Jamboard to add their own responses to the prompts, generating a Jamboard that helped them to understand their own ideas and motivations better by seeing their peers' thought processes.

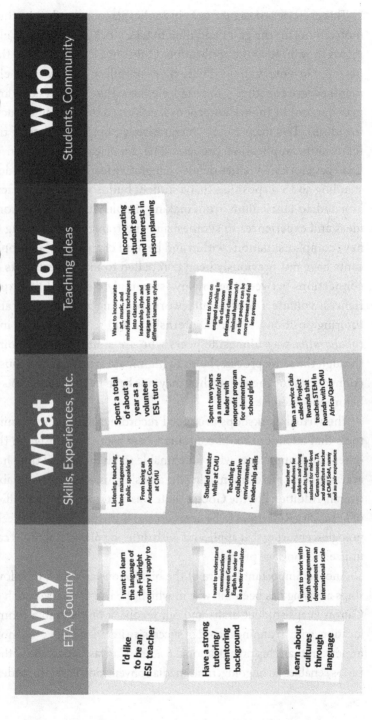

Collaborative Online Pedagogical Strategies

Why	What	How	Who
ETA, Country	Skills, Experiences, etc.	Teaching Ideas	Students, Community

Why (ETA, Country):
- I'd like to be an ESL teacher
- I want to learn the language of the Fulbright country I apply to
- Have a strong tutoring/mentoring background
- I want to understand communication between German & English in order to be a better translator
- Learn about cultures through language
- I want to work with youth engagement/development on an international scale

What (Skills, Experiences, etc.):
- Listening, teaching, time management, public speaking
- From being an Academic Coach at CMU
- Spent a total of about a year as a volunteer ESL tutor
- Studied theater while at CMU
- Teaching in collaborative environments, leadership skills
- Spent two years as a mentor/site leader with nonprofit program for elementary school girls
- Teacher of mindfulness for children and young adults, language assistant for mid-level German classes, TA and substitute teacher at CMU SoM, nanny and au pair experience
- Run a service club called Project Rwanda that teaches STEM in Rwanda with CMU Africa/Qatar

How (Teaching Ideas):
- Want to incorporate art, music, and mindfulness techniques into classroom leadership style and engage students with different learning styles
- Incorporating student goals and interests in lesson planning
- I want to focus on engaged teaching in the classroom (interactive classes with minimal homework) so that people can be more present and feel less pressure

Who (Students, Community)

Figure 9.2. Example of collaboratively generated Google Jamboard from the Fulbright ETA Proposal Workshop. A similar Jamboard frame is utilized in the study/research proposal workshop.

This exercise is designed to help applicants first to reflect on their motivations for the grant and then to take stock of the various elements they bring to the application. Only once they have done this personal inventory do we invite them to reflect on how these elements weave together—for example, how the "what" (skills and experiences) of their ETA proposal relates to their "how" (teaching ideas). This maps to the "integrative learning" outcome of the fellowships application process. The American Association of Colleges and Universities defines integrative learning as "an understanding and a disposition that a student builds across the curriculum and co-curriculum, from making simple connections among ideas and experiences to synthesizing and transferring learning to new, complex situations within and beyond campus."[7] Many applicants have not previously been compelled to make these sorts of connections between their many (seemingly disparate) life experiences: volunteer work, coursework, teaching assistantships and tutoring positions, research, internships, and so on. Doing so in a *collaborative* way, alongside peers who are simultaneously going through the same process, helps to illuminate syntheses and causal connections for them that they may not have been inclined to see before this exercise.

The virtual workshops produced recordings and brainstorming tools that attendees could continue to use asynchronously; on the other hand, applicants who were unable to attend in real time had access to these materials, making the advising process more equitable overall. Additionally, the Google Suite was determined by our Office of Disability Resources to be accessible to those using assistive technologies, ensuring that applicants with differing physical abilities can utilize the tools we provide.

Another important feature of the bichronous approach to fellowships advising has been the way in which the use of an LMS such as Canvas keeps student drafts and our feedback on them in a central location, with a running record of successive iterations. But even more important than this organizational feature, Canvas (along with other LMSs) enables an ongoing, multimedia conversation between student and advisor in a way that sending feedback via email does not. This becomes even more important in the remote, bichronous environment, when engagement is happening across different geographical locations and time zones and around internship, research, vacation, and summer course schedules. With Canvas's capabilities for in-system annotation, video feedback, file attachments, and submission comments, applicants can receive multiple modes of feedback at once and leave their own submission comments in response, opening up a conversation that can bridge real-time meetings (Figure 9.3).

Audience analysis is an additional key aspect of the fellowships application process that can be fruitfully approached with peer-to-peer learning in bichronous pedagogical designs. Regardless of the targeted fellowship, applicants must be taught to consider the balancing act of articulating their own narratives, goals, and motivations while also speaking to the priorities of the funding body. As with other aspects of the application development process, audience analysis can be enhanced when applicants are introduced to its key components in a cohort-based, collaborative setting and then given time to reflect on their own.

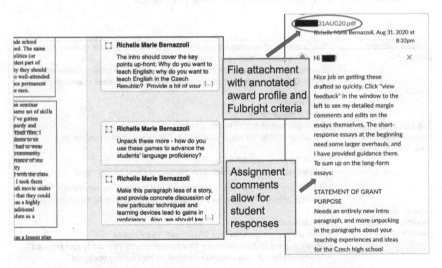

Figure 9.3. Multimodal feedback in Canvas using in-system annotation, file attachments, and submission comments.

Our virtual Fulbright Personal Statement Writing Workshop is held in early June, after the proposal writing workshops and before the first draft deadline (see Figure 9.1). The rationale for this timing is that applicants will have the chance to familiarize themselves with and reflect on the elements of Fulbright proposals before thinking about how they will approach the more personal introduction they will aim to achieve with their personal statements. Figure 9.4 depicts the audience analysis slide shown to participants during the virtual workshop. The workshop facilitator walks through the various levels of reading audience and accompanying considerations. They then give participants time to reflect on and discuss the audience analysis process in virtual breakout rooms. Finally, participants are asked to do a quick-write exercise that helps them to begin weaving their personal inventory together with the priorities of their audience. Because we house the workshop recordings and slide decks together in Canvas, this exercise can easily be done asynchronously by those who are not able to attend in real time. An opportunity for personal statement peer reviews is also facilitated asynchronously via Canvas in order to give applicants additional perspectives on how their narratives are taking shape, and to further learn from one another's writing processes.

What is Fulbright's mission? https://us.fulbrightonline.org/about	"The 'promotion of international good will through the exchange of students in the fields of education, culture, and science.'" "Bilateral relationships in which citizens and governments of other countries work with the U.S. to set joint priorities and shape the program to meet shared needs."
Who is reading the applications at the U.S. level of review?	Study/research: • Country/region experts • For larger countries: STEM-only panels • For arts proposals: Artists in your field and familiar with your host country
	English Teaching assistantship: • ESL experts who are experienced in the targeted host country/region
Who is reading the applications at the host country level of review (for semifinalists)?	• Most likely a mix of academics, government and business representatives, U.S. embassy personnel, and former Fulbrighters from the country to the United States Considerations: • What are key issues in the host country with regard to your field? • What are major priorities/initiatives for your host country relevant to your proposal? • What would be culturally/politically sensitive for host country reviewers?

Figure 9.4. Audience analysis slide from Carnegie Mellon's Fulbright Personal Statement Writing Workshop.

While it is difficult to assess the impact of these bichronous strategies in terms of fellowship outcomes, informal applicant feedback and our own advising experiences have affirmed that our post–March 2020 practices have cultivated a sense of cohort engagement and support that has enhanced the application process. From the advising end, we have been pleased with the continuous connection we feel with applicants throughout the cycle, and the ease of organization and tracking that has been a practical outcome of this approach. We are also heartened by the increased access and equity for applicants who are coming to the process from different backgrounds and circumstances. However, more rigorous assessment is needed, particularly in relation to a codified set of learning outcomes. In the Office of Undergraduate Research and Scholarship Development at Carnegie Mellon University, we have initiated just such an assessment process, which will unfold over the next several years.

Meredith Raucher Sisson, Virginia
Commonwealth University

As we noted earlier, the literature strongly supports a bichronous approach to teaching, and we have found this to be true in fellowships advising at Virginia Commonwealth University as well. As all teaching moved online in March 2020, we too needed to adjust our own classes and advising practices to the online space. At that time, I was teaching a course, How to Apply: Nationally Competitive Awards and Beyond. The messy transition to online demonstrated that digital tools could not quite re-create the classroom experience, but they had the potential to be just as effective. Simply moving my class onto Zoom and hoping I could teach it as I had initially planned it proved unsuccessful. Many students disengaged once they were no longer required to put on pants and show up to a physical space. We all quickly learned the challenge of speaking to a room of black boxes, and many faces turned into still photos—if we were lucky—or simply names. It was impossible to know whether anything was landing with the students, or if they were even sitting at their computers to hear it. Over the course of the semester, I tried out several strategies for online teaching, learning from my more experienced colleagues and relentlessly trying new approaches.

At the time, our campus used Blackboard as its LMS, which was not a particularly nimble tool for me as a novice user, but it gave me the ability to build a resource library for my students and to enable them to share materials with one another for peer review through discussion boards. On Zoom, I started each class meeting with a check-in, in order to help build community and foster belonging. I encouraged use of the chat box to complement (and, for some students, even replace) the live discussions we were having. I began to see that I needed to encourage engagement both in our synchronous meetings and outside class time, with the course materials as well as their classmates.

I was able to take lessons learned from the online classroom into my advising practices. I soon adapted my course material for a workshop series I was going to launch that next spring, primarily targeting upperclassmen, graduate students, and alumni applying for postgraduate and graduate fellowships. Virginia Commonwealth University was then transitioning from Blackboard to Canvas, and I took the opportunity to really learn how to use our new LMS and better implement more of the pedagogical tools on offer for online learning. My workshop participants would meet once a week on Zoom and would find the materials they needed for each week's session built into a module in the Canvas course. This time, however, the LMS would serve as more than just a virtual repository for course materials.

I asked the students to add their contact information and awards of interest to a page in the course as a first step to building a cohort. Beyond each week's check-in, during which I asked participants to share the best thing that had happened for them since the last time we met, I folded the Six-Word Memoir[8] into a multiweek exercise that, after I introduced it in week one, largely took place in a discussion board. In part one, the students were to post a memoir, aiming to offer six words that described them best. In part two, they then needed to find images that they felt best represented two of their peers' memoirs and explain why they felt each image most accurately portrayed what the memoir conveyed. For the final part of the

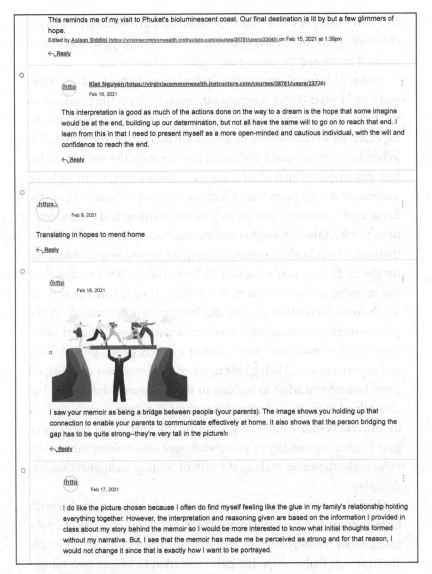

This reminds me of my visit to Phuket's bioluminescent coast. Our final destination is lit by but a few glimmers of hope.
Edited by Aslaan Siddiqi (https://virginiacommonwealth.instructure.com/courses/28781/users/23048) on Feb 15, 2021 at 1:39pm
↩ Reply

Kiet Nguyen (https://virginiacommonwealth.instructure.com/courses/28781/users/23726)
Feb 16, 2021

This interpretation is good as much of the actions done on the way to a dream is the hope that some imagine would be at the end, building up our determination, but not all have the same will to go on to reach that end. I learn from this in that I need to present myself as a more open-minded and cautious individual, with the will and confidence to reach the end.
↩ Reply

(https:
Feb 8, 2021

Translating in hopes to mend home
↩ Reply

(http
Feb 16, 2021

I saw your memoir as being a bridge between people (your parents). The image shows you holding up that connection to enable your parents to communicate effectively at home. It also shows that the person bridging the gap has to be quite strong--they're very tall in the picture.
↩ Reply

(http
Feb 17, 2021

I do like the picture chosen because I often do find myself feeling like the glue in my family's relationship holding everything together. However, the interpretation and reasoning given are based on the information I provided in class about my story behind the memoir so I would be more interested to know what initial thoughts formed without my narrative. But, I see that the memoir has made me be perceived as strong and for that reason, I would not change it since that is exactly how I want to be portrayed.

Figure 9.5. Six-Word Memoir discussion board.

assignment, the original author responded to the choice of image and explanation offered by their peers (Figure 9.5).

This not only gave the participants another opportunity to get to know one another and engage in this community of learners, but it also offered a way to begin exploring how they presented themselves and how those presentations were received. Surrounding each asynchronous piece of the assignment, we would engage in discussion about it in our synchronous meetings.

Inspired by Anne Lamott's *Bird by Bird: Some Instructions on Writing and Life*,[9] I used "short assignments," each built on the previous, to teach the fundamental aspects of a personal statement. In-class writing exercises were bolstered by discussion in the main room as well as in breakout rooms, and I continued to encourage the use of the chat box and emojis, which often resulted in more engagement with the material and with peers than I had ever seen in a classroom, as students kept a running commentary on our learning and offered reactions to each other's thoughts and stories. The cohesion of the group that ensued was both incredibly exciting for me and hugely influential for them. They actually learned the materials better because they felt invested in the success of the others. They learned at least as much from each other as they did from me (if not more). In the post-workshop evaluation, a number of participants offered variations on the sentiment that learning of their peers' perspectives and experiences, and being able to share their own, not only helped them brainstorm what to include in their personal statements but also helped them to understand how their narratives were perceived by others. Perhaps more importantly, the workshop experience gave them a community of peers who were also making themselves vulnerable, therefore making the task of writing an application less daunting.

Over the last few years, I have continued to build and tinker with Canvas courses for several awards that have large cohorts of applicants, most recently for the National Science Foundation Graduate Research Fellowship. The course needed to ensure two things: First, that it could make the information more broadly accessible, in order to support a larger cohort of applicants and also enable more equitable advising, as all students who engage with our process now have access to all the same information. Second, the course needed to guide students through the application process in a way that gave them opportunities to work independently but also to engage with advisors and with other applicants. The bichronous approach worked well.

I intentionally designed this Canvas course—and I do consider it a course—with our learning outcomes in mind. While I aim for students to accomplish all that we listed earlier (award basics, leveraging a network, audience analysis, personal statement as genre, integrative learning, proposal development, collaborative and cohort-based learning), I will outline a few outcomes for consideration here.

My first module covers award basics, providing information about eligibility, benefits, and the application. Applicants are required to either attend a live information session or watch a recording, embedded in this module. Before they can move on to the rest of the course, they must pass a four-question quiz showing they have at least a baseline understanding of the National Science Foundation Graduate Research Fellowship. The next module guides them in leveraging their networks by asking them to provide not only a list of potential recommenders that includes thoughts on what each could write in a letter but also a team roster of those who will support them, in whatever ways they need, through the application process. I aim for them to recognize that the awards office is not their only resource and that others in their networks have a role to play in their success, from brainstorming and draft review to holding them accountable and making sure they take breaks.

There are modules for the personal and research statements, teaching each as genre and as an essay specifically for the Graduate Research Fellowship application. The course also provides opportunities for structured brainstorming, which enables the applicants to think about the full range of their experiences and how they might be leveraged in their essays, as well as for receiving feedback on their written work. Even as the course itself provides asynchronous tools and resources, I incorporate opportunities for cohort building and collaborative learning—for example, through a mandatory "Introduce Yourself" discussion board, which is one of the first tasks they must complete. Canvas also facilitates asynchronous peer review. I provide a worksheet and instructions for the applicants, whom I then pair off directly through the assignment.

Synchronously, I provide applicants their own virtual space on Slack and offer live programming, which is recorded and shared in Canvas for those unable to attend. Such programs include a writing workshop and panel presentations from faculty reviewers and Virginia Commonwealth University students and alumni who hold or have held the award. Applicants also have the chance to meet with a campus review panel, comprising three or four faculty from their (broad) discipline, to get feedback on their materials.

While my experience advising applicants using asynchronous materials coupled with synchronous touchpoints is, at best, a case study or a case in point, I can attest to the impact of bichronous learning, not least of all because it facilitates community. I have observed that students want the ability to work on their own time, but that the touchpoints a bichronous approach affords help them stay motivated and on track. It provides a sense of belonging within the flexibility of asynchronous learning, and that is, in some measure, what keeps them in the process and gets them over the finish line. While we celebrate the submitted application as the tangible accomplishment, we should also recognize the power of bichronous learning, which offers a high-impact practice that has the potential to transform our applicants through community, self-discovery, and concrete skill building.

Conclusion

As the literature suggests and our combined experiences bear out, scholarship applicants have much to gain from engaging in both synchronous and asynchronous learning throughout an application process. The bichronous approach has allowed us to teach to our learning outcomes through fellowships advising and to provide the students and alumni we advise with a transformative experience that empowers them to tell their stories and pursue their futures with confidence, whether or not they receive the award they applied for. Engaging in bichronous learning allows for both flexibility and rigor, meeting many applicants wherever they are, and creates a more accessible and equitable form of advising.

Notes

1. Benjamin Moorehouse and Kevin Wong, "Blending Asynchronous and Synchronous Digital Technologies and Instructional Approaches to Facilitate Remote Learning," *Journal of Computational Education* 9, no. 1 (2022): 51–70; Florence Martin et al., "Bichronous Online Learning: Award-Winning Online Instructor Practices of Blending Asynchronous and Synchronous Online Modalities," *Internet and Higher Education* 56 (2023): 100879; Jesslyn Farros et al., "The Effect of Synchronous Discussion Sessions in an Asynchronous Course," *Journal of Behavioral Education* 31 (2022): 718–30.
2. Martin et al., "Bichronous Online Learning."
3. Adapted from Florence Martin, Drew Polly, and Albert Ritzhaupt, "Bichronous Online Learning: Blending Asynchronous and Synchronous Online Learning," *EDUCAUSE Review*, September 8, 2020, https://er .educause.edu/articles/2020/9/bichronous-online-learning-blending -asynchronous-and-synchronous-online-learning.
4. Martin, Polly, and Ritzhaupt.
5. Farros et al., "Effect of Synchronous Discussion"; Martin et al., "Bichronous Online Learning."
6. Mehmet Kara, "Revisiting Online Learner Engagement: Exploring the Role of Learner Characteristics in an Emergency Period," *Journal of Research on Technology in Education* 54, no. 1 (2021): 236–52.
7. "Integrative and Applied Learning VALUE Rubric," American Association of Colleges and Universities, https://www.aacu.org/initiatives/value -initiative/value-rubrics/value-rubrics-integrative-and-applied-learning.
8. Six-Word Memoirs, https://www.sixwordmemoirs.com.
9. Anne Lamott, *Bird by Bird: Some Instructions on Writing and Life* (New York: Anchor Books, 2019).

10

Fellowships in Support of Graduate Professionalization

MATTHEW KLOPFENSTEIN

The state and future of graduate education has become a topic of growing debate in higher education in recent years, with many calling for a fundamental reimagining of graduate training to address concerns about cost, time to degree, and uncertain career outcomes. The foreword to a recent volume on graduate student support captures the current mood, noting, "The shortcomings of graduate education are becoming more apparent to many observers, faculty members, leaders, researchers, and students."[1] As staff typically not associated with a particular academic program or unit, graduate fellowships advisors contribute to institutional efforts to provide support for graduate students beyond their disciplines and degree programs, and we have a role to play in promoting and developing efforts to address current challenges and needs in graduate education.

Career preparation and professional development have emerged as a particular focus within the growing number of works stressing the need to reform and reimagine graduate training.[2] This focus is reflected in major grant-funded initiatives aimed at improving graduate education, such as the Council of Graduate Schools (CGS) PhD Career Pathways project.[3] These efforts come at a time when many institutions are already substantially increasing their investment in programming and services for graduate career preparation.[4] At the same time, researchers have noted that support for graduate students has often been delivered as an extension of existing programs and services for undergraduates without serious engagement with the ways in which the needs and experiences of graduate students differ from those of undergraduates.[5] There is consequently a need for higher education professionals who work primarily with graduate students to help shape institutional efforts to develop and deliver graduate student services, particularly in the area of professional development.

Fellowships advising is an overlooked area of research on graduate student services.[6] However, the growing attention to professional development within larger conversations on the direction of graduate education has important implications for the ways in which graduate fellowships advisors understand our work and communicate its significance to both the students we support and the broader community of graduate education stakeholders. As institutions and graduate students place more emphasis on career preparation and professionalization, it is crucial that fellowships advisors understand how our work relates to these ends, as we seek to best support students, while also clearly articulating our contribution to the larger missions of the institutions we serve.

National Association of Fellowships Advisors graduate fellowships advisors at a variety of institutions are already active in these efforts, developing skills-focused programming through certification programs, courses, boot camps, and other trainings that stress the professional development value of fellowships applications.[7] At the same time, graduate fellowships advising is situated in a variety of contexts across and within institutions. Fellowships advisors working primarily or exclusively with graduate students work in offices that may be administratively located in a graduate college, provost's office, office of research, or office of professional development. At my own institution, the University of South Carolina, the National Fellowships and Scholar Programs office is administratively located in the South Carolina Honors College, even though it serves students in all programs and at all levels. Advisors whose offices are not administratively located in graduate-focused units or who are at institutions with less robust graduate student services may have more limited access to conversations on graduate student support. In all cases, however, a focus on professional development can provide a way of connecting our efforts as fellowships advisors with pressing concerns in graduate education and may serve as a useful way to bring visibility to this work.

My aim here is to emphasize the professional development value of the work currently being done by graduate fellowships advisors and connect these efforts with research on graduate student professionalization to suggest how a greater emphasis on the professional development value of fellowships can provide new ways of approaching programming and campus partnerships. To that end, I offer an overview of current research on graduate student professional development and provide an example from my own institution of a recent attempt to make fellowships more central to graduate professional development efforts. The Graduate Student Resources Hub, or Grad Hub, a new initiative at the University of South Carolina developed in a partnership between the Graduate School, Career Center, and National Fellowships Office, serves as a case study of what this might look like from a programming and messaging standpoint. This attempt to provide a wider platform for graduate fellowships advising through a focus on professional development may serve as a generative example for fellowships advisors looking to create or expand their own programming and campus collaborations.

Graduate Student Professional Development: Background, Definitions, and Relevance to Fellowships

Institutional interest in graduate student professional development has grown over the last several decades. Graduate professional development initiatives in the United States aimed at helping students identify and develop skills applicable to a variety of career paths are a direct result of efforts to restructure doctoral education in the face of an increasingly competitive academic job market. This work can be traced back in part to the 1990s and early 2000s, when organizations like the National Academies, Pew Charitable Trust, and Carnegie Foundation undertook major studies of PhD education "with a particular focus on career preparation."[8] More recently, major disciplinary associations such as the American Historical Association and Modern Language Association, as well as higher education professional organizations like the Graduate Careers Consortium, have undertaken a series of initiatives aimed at reforming graduate education with an eye to improved and diversified career outcomes.[9]

While a need for professional development is widely recognized, a clear consensus has yet to emerge on its precise definition in the context of graduate education.[10] Maresi Nerad has drawn a distinction between "PhD-completion skills" and "professional skills," with the latter encompassing "career competencies beyond traditional academic skills."[11] Ariana Garcia and Enyu Zhou bring both sets of skills under the umbrella of "professional development," distinguishing between "academic PD," which "focuses on skills related to the academic portion of the PhD," and "other PD," which encompasses "interpersonal skills like leadership, networking, [and] public speaking."[12] This approach is present in the results of a 2013 study of graduate student attitudes toward professional development, which found that participants viewed professional development in terms of both academic and career preparation.[13] While still delineating specific professional skills, Radomir Ray Mitic and Hironao Okahana have framed professional development in terms of "structured experiences" and training "beyond coursework and the dissertation."[14] Despite these variations in terminology and emphasis, a clear focus on skills and experiences applicable to a variety of career paths is the common thread running through these definitions, as is a recognition that professional development opportunities may come from beyond a student's academic program or department.

However professional development is defined, there is significant overlap with the skills that graduate fellowships advisors seek to foster and those most commonly identified as important to career preparation in research on graduate students. As advisors we are used to emphasizing the value of the fellowship application process as a developmental activity that can help to clarify ideas, articulate long-term goals, improve research communication, and learn a particular form of academic writing.[15] These skills are relevant both to degree completion and to career development. Furthermore, they relate to a number of professional development activities that PhD alumni identified as useful in response to a 2020 CGS survey that was part of the larger Understanding PhD Career Pathways for Program Improvement project.[16] Communication, academic writing, leadership development, grant writing, research or fieldwork abroad, and diversity, equity, and inclusion competency stand out among the seventeen total activities noted in responses for their relevance to the process of applying for external funding opportunities or to features of fellowship programs that graduate advisors frequently promote.[17]

There is a clear case to be made that our work as fellowships advisors furthers graduate student professional development and positively contributes to the career outcomes of our students. Grant writing, the skill arguably most directly related to our work, has been identified as a particularly valuable professional competency by PhD alumni working inside and beyond academia.[18] CGS's Humanities Coalition, a career preparation initiative funded by the Mellon Foundation, has among its aims to "generate promising practices for institutions seeking to develop or augment professional development programs in grant writing."[19] Additionally, the process of applying for a fellowship relates directly to three of the four aspects of research communication that postdoctoral participants in CGS's PhD alumni survey used to evaluate their training: "communicating ideas clearly and persuasively in writing, such as journal articles, grant proposals, or reports"; "communicating ideas clearly and persuasively to a variety of audiences who may not have technical backgrounds about your field of PhD"; and "grant writing."[20]

At the same time, researchers have noted discrepancies between students' reported interest in professional development opportunities and their actual participation in these activities.[21] Sara Cavallo and colleagues caution that meeting graduate student professional development needs will not likely be achieved by simply offering more programming, as many institutions already provide a wide range of (at times overlapping) opportunities at the level of individual programs, disciplines, and support offices. The challenge, then, becomes how to help students navigate these various options and understand what value they might offer.[22] Clear communication about, and contextualization of, professional development activities is consequently key to supporting graduate students.

The significant interest in graduate student professional development and its demonstrated impact on students suggest that fellowships advisors have an interest in positioning our work as a contribution to this both in our interactions with students and in how we communicate the nature and impact of our work to our larger institutions. Presenting the application for a fellowship as an important part of graduate training and professional preparation allows us to frame our work in terms that are increasingly valued by institutions and students alike. However, this framing goes beyond simply drawing attention to the specific skills and learning outcomes associated with applying for fellowships. It also suggests that graduate advisors should consider approaching the programming that we offer in ways that explicitly connect with key professional development skills valued by our students and recent alumni.

Such framing may be useful in increasing access to fellowship opportunities for students from historically underrepresented backgrounds as well. A recent CGS analysis of PhD students in life and health sciences, physical and earth sciences, engineering, math, and computer science found that women and underrepresented minorities (defined by the survey as "American Indian/Alaska Native, Black/African American, Hispanic, and Native Hawaiian and Pacific Islander" doctoral students) showed greater rates of participation than male, white, and Asian students in all eight areas of professional development considered: career preparation, academic writing, digital literacy, research ethics, quantitative literacy, teaching preparation, project management, and grant writing. The largest participation disparities were in the areas of academic writing, project management, and grant writing, all areas with strong relevance to fellowship applications.[23] Tailoring fellowships programming and the way that we advertise it to connect with these particular skills may help advisors reach a wider range of student populations and allow us to serve students whose degree programs or other factors, such as citizenship status, might otherwise limit options for external funding, including students enrolled in master's and professional programs and international students.

Case Study: The Graduate Student Resources Hub at the University of South Carolina

The Grad Hub at the University of South Carolina is one example of how graduate fellowships advising can play a role in developing graduate student services and promoting professionalization at an institution where fellowships advising is not administratively tied to a unit primarily focused on graduate students. The Grad Hub is a multiunit collaboration initiated by National Fellowships with the Career Center and Graduate School that developed from an eight-person working group over the course of 2021. The Grad Hub reflects growing institutional efforts to improve graduate student services that included hiring the first graduate fellowships and graduate career advisor in 2021.

As a collaboration between three different units on campus, the Grad Hub allows each partner office to help shape the identity and mission of the space, while in turn letting that larger purpose influence our individual approach to messaging and programming. This has allowed National Fellowships to develop a distinct identity for graduate student advising in an office that primarily serves undergraduates through close collaboration with other key graduate studies stakeholders. Under the aegis of the Grad Hub, I have been able to develop outreach messaging and programming for graduate fellowships that complements the student services and career-planning work of our partners in the Graduate School and Career Center without duplicating programs and services that are already provided.

The Grad Hub's mission is "to provide a more integrated graduate student experience that holistically encompasses academic training and professional development for students" at the University of South Carolina.[24] It encompasses both a modest physical space, formally launched in March 2022, and a larger internal brand for graduate professional development activities. The physical space currently houses graduate career and fellowships advisors, a common work area, and a classroom for events. Through a regular newsletter, weekly professional development announcements, and a slate of professional development workshops, the Grad Hub seeks to provide more cohesive communication about graduate professional development activities while offering a mix of programming from a variety of support offices and units. Our approach seeks to further validate Mariann Sanchez and Trista Beard's claim that "cross-unit collaborations to design intentional programs and workshops have proven successful in improving communication and overall systems of support" for graduate students.[25]

The Grad Hub also plays a role in graduate student recruitment and orientation. Representatives from the Graduate School, National Fellowships, and the Career Center meet regularly to coordinate programming and outreach and present together for graduate student orientations hosted by specific programs, allowing students to see fellowships advising as one of the key supports available to them on campus. Additionally, the Grad Hub has done presentations for faculty on graduate student services. We have also presented to prospective students on campus visits and participated in recruitment programming hosted by other groups on campus. These sessions allow students to encounter graduate fellowships advising at the very start of their programs as a core student service.

The Grad Hub provides both space and branding for hosting fellowships and fellowships-adjacent workshops that encourage students to see fellowship and grant applications in the context of research communication, professional development planning, and academic writing. The fellowships office spearheaded the development of a newsletter for the Grad Hub, designing it and compiling content for each issue. Since the Graduate School does not currently send out a regular newsletter, this addresses an important communication gap with graduate students and has given us the opportunity to shape campus-wide messaging around graduate student professional development. This newsletter, sent to the more than six thousand graduate students at the university, provides a much wider audience for graduate fellowships than our separate, opt-in graduate fellowships newsletter. The goal is to present applying for fellowships as a professional development activity alongside more conventionally career-oriented programming like sessions on résumé and CV preparation, interviews, and salary negotiation.

Our monthly newsletter features recent articles from outlets like *Inside Higher Ed* and the *Chronicle of Higher Education* on career preparation, a monthly professional development tip using the hashtag #gradprofdev that the Graduate School uses for its social media outreach, upcoming programming offered by National Fellowships and the Career Center aimed at graduate students, and information on relevant opportunities from partner offices on campus. By bringing together offerings from other units that are not formally part of the Grad Hub but offer professional development programming, such as the Writing Center and Center for Teaching Excellence, we seek to complement and amplify the work of campus partners and signal the professional development value of their resources, while also addressing a challenge faced by many institutions: "Various departments, college-level units and university-level units offer sometimes-overlapping programs but graduate students are often left to their own devices in finding out what programs exist, what value they potentially bring and how to access them."[26]

The Grad Hub initiative has allowed me to think about how, as a graduate fellowships advisor, I can translate the skills and learning involved in fellowships applications to a broader audience of students, while still providing focused fellowships support. Through the Grad Hub I have developed a series of fellowships-specific and fellowships-adjacent programming. I offer a regular series of fellowships-focused workshops that include an introduction to graduate fellowships and writing fellowships in STEM and humanities and social sciences disciplines. Beyond these more traditional fellowships topics, I have also developed three workshops specifically for the Grad Hub's mission aimed at larger professional development skills that also serve to introduce students to the world of external fellowships: Applying to PhD Programs, Planning Your Graduate Experience, and Communicating Your Scholarly Identity and Research Agenda. These workshops are meant to promote professional development in the broad sense of developing specific skills around planning, project management, and research communication, while also encouraging general student success by working to make visible aspects of the hidden curriculum of graduate school.[27]

These interactive sessions allow for sharing information about fellowships as one part of a larger process of graduate professional development. For example, the Applying to PhD Programs workshop, which is aimed at current master's students, provides an overview of the different aspects of doctoral education funding. This presentation includes a discussion of different types of external funding as well as an overview of useful databases for finding graduate funding. Planning Your Graduate Experience uses a backward design approach to teach students to construct a multiyear plan for meeting personal, academic, and professional development milestones based on the CV or résumé that students wish to have when they finish their programs. In this context I discuss the value of applying for fellowships and a timeline for what this might look like in a graduate program alongside other activities like scholarly publications and conference presentations. Similarly, in Communicating Your Scholarly Identity and Research Agenda, I lead students through guided reflections based in part on M. F. Price's Scholarly Identity Mapping exercises to help clarify key motivations and commitments in a student's scholarship and professional goals that can then be deployed in a variety of ways, including through use in job materials and fellowship applications.[28] The emphasis is on developing research communication skills, with fellowships featured as one potential application among many.

Beyond providing programming on topics that are not otherwise covered by other units on campus, the goal for these sessions is not to use them as a direct recruitment tool for fellowship applicants but rather to make clear to graduate students that applying for external funding is a beneficial (and in many cases expected) activity that should be seriously considered as part of their studies. These workshops have only been offered a limited number of times, and it remains to be seen what impact they might have on how graduate students see fellowships in terms of professional development.

However, student feedback as provided through assessment surveys has been overwhelmingly positive, with respondents particularly emphasizing that they found the information and activities in the sessions practical and actionable.

The Grad Hub, having only been operating for one full academic year at the time of writing, is very much a work in progress. This past year has been focused on identifying student needs and interests and building recognition for the initiative among students, faculty, and administrators. We are still experimenting with outreach efforts and programming formats, and it is too early to offer any definite conclusions about the impact of this work. One challenge we have faced is a low conversion rate of registrants for workshops to those who actually attend sessions. This may reflect graduate students' general interest in professional development programming but preference for options sponsored by their own programs as opposed to those provided by other units.[29] To address this, we are currently working on partnering with other units on campus that offer professional development programming to include our sessions in their series, and we will be prioritizing the delivery of tailored versions of our programming for specific departments and degree programs in the coming year.

Meeting the needs of graduate students at a time when many are debating the need for substantial changes in the way graduate education is conceived and delivered requires flexibility and experimentation, and I present the programming and outreach that I have offered through the Grad Hub as an evolving effort to feature fellowship applications foremost as a professional development activity. By providing concrete examples, I aim to encourage other graduate fellowships advisors to explore what this might look like in their own institutional context in order to reflect more on the distinct obstacles and opportunities available to them and to build a larger body of knowledge of successful practices.

Conclusion

The growing attention to career preparation in graduate education provides both opportunities and challenges for graduate fellowships advisors. Applying for fellowships is an activity that encompasses both the academic and career-preparatory aspects of graduate professional development. It is a form of academic training that can aid in progress to degree and an activity that involves transferable skills in areas like grant writing and research communication. While fellowships support is often listed on professional development resource webpages for graduate schools, this suggests that fellowships advising deserves to be featured alongside explicitly skill-oriented workshops, certificate programs, and special events for graduate students whenever possible. This is not to say that graduate fellowships advisors should feel compelled to expand the scope of their work or take on new, time-intensive projects that may be tangential to the expressed missions of their offices. Institutions vary widely in the kind of programming and support already offered to their graduate students, and fellowships advisors may not always be best positioned to offer additional professional development support beyond their specific fellowships duties. However, even in those cases advisors may still benefit from thinking of their work as supporting professional development.

A focus on professional development provides an additional way to communicate the value of graduate fellowships advising to students and administrators. At the same time, it challenges advisors to think about how to enhance the professional development value of the advising and programming that we offer. This might mean a different approach to how fellowships services are advertised or a more explicit focus on transferable learning outcomes from our workshops, boot camps, and advising appointments. Or it might entail seeking out other units on campus to collaborate with on events and programming under the banner of graduate professional development or focusing on a more specific aspect like research communication or grant writing. At a higher level, it might mean that National Association of Fellowships Advisors members seek out opportunities to collaborate with other professional organizations like the Graduate Career Consortium or the CGS to make sure that our work is better represented in current discussions about graduate education and its outcomes. This is a topic worthy of further exploration, and my hope is that this essay can serve as a starting point for identifying key issues and opportunities for graduate fellowships advising to make our voices heard in discussions on graduate education and graduate student services both in the context of our own distinct institutions and as a larger group of higher education professionals.

Notes

1. Ann E. Austin, foreword to *A Handbook for Supporting Today's Graduate Students*, ed. David J. Nguyen and Christina W. Yao (Sterling, VA: Stylus, 2022), xi.
2. Alan I. Leshner and Layne Scherer, eds., *Graduate STEM Education for the 21st Century* (Washington, DC: National Academies Press, 2018); Katina L. Rogers, *Putting the Humanities PhD to Work: Thriving in and beyond the Classroom* (Durham, NC: Duke University Press, 2020); Leonard Cassuto and Robert Weisbuch, *The New PhD: How to Build a Better Graduate Education* (Baltimore: Johns Hopkins University Press, 2021).
3. "PhD Career Pathways," Council of Graduate Schools, https://cgsnet.org /project/understanding-phd-career-pathways-for-program-improvement/.
4. Jake Livengood, "Exploring the Role of Graduate Student Career Development in Higher Education: How Resources Evolved," in Nguyen and Yao, *Handbook*, 181–82.
5. Katherine Hall-Hertel, Lisa C. O. Brandes, and Valerie A. Shepard, "Introduction: Context, Research, and Application," in *A Practitioner's Guide to Supporting Graduate and Professional Students*, ed. Valerie A. Shepard and April L. Perry (New York: Routledge, 2022), 3–16; Mariann Sanchez and Trista Beard, "Graduate Student Engagement and Campus Programming," in Shepard and Perry, *Practitioner's Guide*, 142–43.
6. Fellowships in general are not addressed in two recent collections on graduate education: Shepard and Perry, *Practitioner's Guide*; and Nguyen and Yao, *Handbook*. Additionally, the National Association of Fellowships Advisors is not included in a list of professional associations with sections devoted to graduate and professional students in Shepard and Perry, *Practitioner's Guide*, 245–47.
7. Beth Keithly et al., "Using Fellowships to Provide Student Professional Development" (virtual presentation at the National Association of Fellowships Advisors Biennial Conference, July 13–15, 2021).
8. Maresi Nerad, "Professional Development for Doctoral Students: What Is It? Why Now? Who Does It?," *Nagoya Journal of Higher Education* 15

(2015): 295–98, direct quotation on 297; Cassuto and Weisbuch, *New PhD*, 37–68.

9. Cassuto and Weisbuch, *New PhD*, 69–90.
10. Nerad, "Professional Development," 287–94; Sonja Rizzolo et al., "Graduate Student Perceptions and Experiences of Professional Development Activities," *Journal of Career Development* 43, no. 3 (June 1, 2016): 195–96; Sara E. Cavallo et al., "Through Many Doors at Once: Rethinking the Multiverse of Graduate Student Professional Development," *Studies in Graduate and Postdoctoral Education* 14, no. 3 (published ahead of print, January 1, 2023): 2–3.
11. Nerad, "Professional Development," 288–89, 300.
12. Ariana L. Garcia and Enyu Zhou, "Academic Professional Development for PhD Students in Selected Science Fields: Who Is Participating?," CGS Research in Brief, Council of Graduate Schools, October 2022, 1.
13. Rizzolo et al., "Graduate Student Perceptions," 202–3.
14. Radomir Ray Mitic and Hironao Okahana, "PhD Professional Development: Value, Timing, and Participation," CGS Research in Brief, Council of Graduate Schools, January 2021, 1.
15. "Tips for Professionals," National Association of Fellowships Advisors, November 22, 2021, https://www.nafadvisors.org/resources/tips-for-professionals/.
16. Mitic and Okahana, "PhD Professional Development," 1.
17. Mitic and Okahana, 2.
18. Ahjah M. Johnson and Enyu Zhou, "Closing Gaps in Our Knowledge of PhD Career Pathways: The Importance of Preparation in Grant Writing for PhDs," CGS Research in Brief, Council of Graduate Schools, August 2022.
19. Johnson and Zhou, 3.
20. Johnson and Zhou, 3. Additionally, the fourth aspect, "communicating ideas clearly and persuasively when speaking to others one-on-one or in small groups," is relevant to those applying to opportunities that use interviews in their evaluation process.
21. Mitic and Okahana, "PhD Professional Development"; Cavallo et al., "Through Many Doors," 1–2.
22. Cavallo et al., "Through Many Doors," 12–13.
23. Garcia and Zhou, "Academic Professional Development," 1–2.
24. "Graduate Student Resources Hub," University of South Carolina, https://www.sc.edu/study/colleges_schools/graduate_school/opportunities_support/the_grad_hub/.
25. Sanchez and Beard, "Graduate Student Engagement," 122.

26. Cavallo et al., "Through Many Doors," 12–13.

27. In doing so I draw on resources like Jessica McCrory Calarco, *A Field Guide to Grad School: Uncovering the Hidden Curriculum* (Princeton, NJ: Princeton University Press, 2020); and Genevieve Negrón-Gonzales and Magdalena L. Barrera, *The Latinx Guide to Graduate School* (Durham, NC: Duke University Press, 2023).

28. Mary F. Price, *Scholarly/Professional Identity Mapping (SIM)*, January 28, 2019, https://scholarworks.iupui.edu/handle/1805/26560.

29. Garcia and Zhou, "Academic Professional Development," 4.

American India Foundation
American-Scandinavian Foundation
American Society for Engineering Education
Amgen Foundation (Harvard University)
Asia Foundation
Astronaut Scholarship Foundation
Bulgarian-American Fulbright Commission
Bureau of Educational and Cultural Affairs (ECA)
Carnegie Endowment for International Peace/James C. Gaither
    Junior Fellows Program
College Track
Cultural Vistas
DAAD German Academic Exchange Service
English-Speaking Union of the United States
Foreign Affairs Information Technology Fellowship and William D.
    Clarke, Sr. Diplomatic Security Fellowship
Fulbright Commission Hungary
FWD: Scholars
Gates Cambridge
General David H. Petraeus Center for Emerging Leaders
Goldwater Scholarship Foundation
Harry S. Truman Scholarship Foundation
Henry Luce Foundation
Hertz Foundation
Honor Society of Phi Kappa Phi
IIE
IIE—Boren Awards
IIE—Fulbright US Student Program
IIE—Gilman International Program
Institute of Current World Affairs
Jack Kent Cooke Foundation
James Madison Memorial Fellowship Foundation
Knight-Hennessy Scholars, Stanford University
Krell Institute/DOE Computational Science Graduate Fellowship
Legacy Award of the Victims of Pan Am Flight 103, Inc.
Marshall Aid Commemoration Commission

McCall MacBain Scholarships at McGill
Meridian International Center
Morris K. Udall and Stewart L. Udall Foundation
NAACP LDF—Marshall-Motley Scholars Program
National Oceanic and Atmospheric Administration
National Science Foundation
NIH/NIAID
Oak Ridge National Laboratory
Pat Tillman Foundation
Paul and Daisy Soros Fellowships for New Americans
Payne Fellowship Program
Posse Foundation
Princeton in Asia
Project Horseshoe Farm
Projects for Peace
Public Policy and International Affairs Program
Rangel Fellowship, Howard University
Rhodes Trust
Rotary Foundation of Rotary International
Schmidt Futures
Schwarzman Scholars
Thomas R. Pickering Fellowship
US Department of State
US-Ireland Alliance
US-UK Fulbright Commission
Vaclav Havel Library Foundation
Watson Foundation
Winston Churchill Foundation of the United States

UK Members
British Council—Study UK
Durham University
Imperial College London
Queen's University Belfast
University College London
University of Bristol

University of Cambridge
University of Manchester
University of Nottingham
University of Sheffield
University of Southampton
University of Sussex
University of Warwick

University Members

Adelphi University
Allegheny College
Alma College
American University
American University in Cairo
Amherst College
Appalachian State University
Arizona State University
Arizona State University Graduate College
Arkansas State University
Auburn University
Augsburg University
Babson College
Ball State University
Bard College
Barnard College
Baruch College, CUNY
Bates College
Baylor University
Beloit College
Bennington College
Binghamton University
Boise State University
Boston University
Bowdoin College
Brandeis University
Bridgewater State University

Brigham Young University
Brown University
Bryn Mawr College
Bucknell University
Butler University
California Institute of Technology
California State University, East Bay
California State University, Fullerton
California State University, Monterey Bay
Carleton College
Carnegie Mellon University
Catholic University of America
Central College
Central Michigan University
Centre College
Chapman University
Christendom College
Citadel
City College of New York–CUNY
Claremont McKenna College
Clarkson University
Clemson University
Coastal Carolina University
Coe College
Coker University
Colby College
Colgate University
College of Charleston
College of New Jersey
College of Saint Benedict/Saint John's University
College of Staten Island
College of the Holy Cross
College of William & Mary
Colorado College
Colorado School of Mines
Colorado State University

Columbia University
Concordia College
Connecticut College
Cornell College
Cornell University
Dartmouth College
Davidson College
Denison University
Dickinson College
Doane University
Dominican University
Drake University
Drexel University
Drury University
Duke Kunshan University
Duke University
Duquesne University
East Carolina University
East Tennessee State University
Eastern Connecticut State University
Eastern Kentucky University
Eastern Michigan University
Eckerd College
Elizabethtown College
Elmhurst University
Elon University
Embry-Riddle Aeronautical University
Emerson College
Emmanuel College
Emory University
Fairfield University
Florida Atlantic University
Florida Gulf Coast University
Florida International University
Florida State University
Fordham University

Fort Hays State University
Franklin & Marshall College
Furman University
George Mason University
George Washington University
Georgetown University
Georgia College and State University
Georgia Institute of Technology
Georgia State University
Grand Valley State University
Grinnell College
Gustavus Adolphus College
Hamilton College
Hampden-Sydney College
Hanover College
Harding University
Harvard College
Harvard Law School
Harvard University
Hastings College
Haverford College
Hobart and William Smith Colleges
Hope College
Hunter College
Indiana University, Bloomington
Iowa State University
Jackson State University
James Madison University
Johns Hopkins University
Juniata College
Kalamazoo College
Kansas State University
Kean University
Kennesaw State University
Kent State
Kenyon College

Knox College
Lafayette College
Lawrence University
Lebanon Valley College
Lehigh University
Le Moyne College
Lewis & Clark College
Liberty University
Louisiana State University
Loyola Marymount University
Loyola University Chicago
Loyola University Maryland
Loyola University New Orleans
Lubbock Christian University
Luther College
Macalester College
Manhattan College
Marist College
Marquette University
Marshall University
Massachusetts Institute of Technology
Mercer University
Miami University
Michigan State University
Middlebury College
Middle Tennessee State University
Millsaps College
Minnesota State University, Mankato
Mississippi State University
Mississippi Valley State University
Monmouth University
Montclair State University
Montgomery College
Morgan State University
Mount Holyoke College
Mount Saint Mary's University, Maryland

Mount Saint Mary's University, Pennsylvania
Muhlenberg College
Murray State University
New College of Florida
New Jersey Institute of Technology
New Mexico State University
New York University
New York University Abu Dhabi
New York University Shanghai
North Carolina Agricultural and Technical State University
North Carolina Central University
North Carolina State University
Northeast Modern Language Association–University at Buffalo
Northeastern University
Northern Arizona University
Northern Illinois University
Northwestern University
Oberlin College
Occidental College
Ohio Northern University
Ohio State University
Ohio University
Oklahoma State University
Oregon Institute of Technology
Oregon State University
Pace University
Pacific Lutheran University
Penn State Erie, The Behrend College
Penn State University
Pierce College
Pitzer College
Pomona College
Portland State University
Pratt Institute
Princeton University
Providence College

Purdue University
Queens College, CUNY
Queens University of Charlotte
Ramapo College
Reed College
Rensselaer Polytechnic Institute
Rhode Island School of Design
Rhodes College
Rice University
Ringling College of Art and Design
Roanoke College
Robert Morris University
Rochester Institute of Technology
Rollins College
Rowan University
Rutgers, the State University of New Jersey
Rutgers University–Camden
Rutgers University–Newark
Saint Joseph's University
Saint Louis University
Salem College
Salisbury University
Salve Regina University
San Diego State University
San Francisco State University
Santa Clara University
Scripps College
Seattle University
Siena College
Simmons University
Skidmore College
Slippery Rock University
Smith College
Southern Arkansas University
Southern Illinois University, Carbondale
Southern Methodist University

Southwestern University
Spelman College
Stanford University
St. Catherine University
St. Edward's University
Stetson University
St. John's College, Annapolis
St. Lawrence University
St. Olaf College
Stonehill College
Stony Brook University (SUNY)
Suffolk University
SUNY Geneseo
SUNY New Paltz
SUNY Old Westbury
SUNY Oswego
Susquehanna University
Swarthmore College
Syracuse University
Tarleton State University
Temple University
Tennessee Tech University
Texas A&M University
Texas A&M University–Kingsville
Texas Christian University
Texas State University
Texas Tech University
Texas Woman's University
Towson University
Transylvania University
Trinity College
Truman State University
Tufts University
Tulane University
Union College
United States Air Force Academy

University at Albany, SUNY
University at Buffalo, SUNY
University of Alabama
University of Alabama at Birmingham
University of Alabama in Huntsville
University of Arizona
University of Arkansas
University of Arkansas at Pine Bluff
University of California, Berkeley
University of California, Davis
University of California, Irvine
University of California, Los Angeles
University of California, Riverside
University of California, Santa Barbara
University of California, Santa Cruz
University of Central Arkansas
University of Central Florida
University of Chicago
University of Cincinnati
University of Colorado Boulder
University of Connecticut
University of Dallas
University of Dayton
University of Delaware
University of Denver
University of Florida
University of Georgia
University of Hawaii at Manoa
University of Houston
University of Idaho
University of Illinois at Chicago
University of Illinois at Urbana Champaign
University of Iowa
University of Kansas
University of Kansas Medical Center

University of Kentucky
University of Louisville
University of Lynchburg
University of Maine
University of Maryland, Baltimore County
University of Maryland, College Park
University of Massachusetts Amherst
University of Massachusetts Boston
University of Massachusetts Lowell
University of Miami
University of Michigan, Ann Arbor
University of Minnesota
University of Minnesota Rochester
University of Minnesota, Twin Cities
University of Mississippi
University of Missouri
University of Missouri–St. Louis
University of Montana
University of Nebraska–Lincoln
University of Nebraska Omaha
University of Nevada Las Vegas
University of Nevada, Reno
University of New Hampshire
University of New Mexico
University of North Alabama
University of North Carolina at Chapel Hill
University of North Carolina at Charlotte
University of North Carolina at Greensboro
University of North Carolina at Wilmington
University of North Carolina School of the Arts
University of North Dakota
University of Northern Iowa
University of North Florida
University of North Georgia
University of North Texas

University of Notre Dame
University of Notre Dame, The Graduate School
University of Oklahoma
University of Oregon
University of Pennsylvania
University of Pittsburgh
University of Pittsburgh at Johnstown
University of Portland
University of Puget Sound
University of Rhode Island
University of Richmond
University of Rochester
University of San Diego
University of South Alabama
University of South Carolina
University of South Dakota
University of Southern California
University of Southern Indiana
University of Southern Mississippi
University of South Florida
University of Tennessee at Chattanooga
University of Tennessee, Knoxville
University of Texas at Austin
University of Texas at Dallas
University of Texas at El Paso
University of Texas at San Antonio
University of Texas Rio Grande Valley
University of the Pacific
University of Toledo
University of Tulsa
University of Utah
University of Vermont
University of Virginia
University of Virginia's College at Wise
University of Washington

University of Washington Bothell
University of West Georgia
University of Wisconsin–Green Bay
University of Wisconsin–Madison
University of Wyoming
Ursinus College
US Coast Guard Academy
USMA West Point
Utah State University
Valparaiso University
Vanderbilt University
Vassar College
Villanova University
Virginia Commonwealth University
Virginia Military Institute
Virginia Tech University
Wabash College
Wake Forest University
Wartburg College
Washington and Lee University
Washington College
Washington State University
Washington University in St. Louis
Wayne State University
Wellesley College
Wesleyan University
Western Carolina University
Western Kentucky University
Western Washington University
Westminster College
West Texas A&M University
West Virginia University
Wheaton College
Whitman College
Wilkes University

Williams College
Winona State University
Winthrop University
Wofford College
Worcester Polytechnic Institute
Xavier University of Louisiana
Yale University

Cassidy Alvarado has served as the director of the Office of National and International Fellowships at Loyola Marymount University (LMU) since 2017. Alvarado is also a lecturer in LMU's Honors Program and currently serves as the communications director for the National Association of Fellowships Advisors (NAFA). Her areas of interest include equity, access, and inclusion in international education; community college and transfer student support; and postgraduate pathways. In June 2022, Alvarado received a Fulbright International Education Administrator Award to South Korea, where she learned about the Korean higher education system through visits to universities and government agencies. Alvarado graduated in May 2021 with her doctorate in educational leadership for social justice from LMU. Her dissertation explored community college and transfer student access to nationally competitive awards. Previously she earned a master's in humanities from Mount Saint Mary's University and a bachelor's in English from the University of Minnesota, Twin Cities.

Richelle Bernazzoli is the director of the Office of Undergraduate Research and Scholar Development at Carnegie Mellon University. She is a political geographer who has taught and written on the topics of militarism, security and identity, and southeastern Europe. She received a 2011–12 Fulbright grant to Croatia for her research on the Euro-Atlantic integration process. Bernazzoli has developed programming to help undergraduate researchers build transferable skills in research design, research communication, and interdisciplinary collaboration. Her current research interests include the development of researcher identity in undergraduate researchers, as well as fellowships applications as a high-impact educational practice. Before joining Carnegie Mellon, Bernazzoli was visiting faculty in the Department of Geography and Geographic Information Science,

University of Illinois, where she taught courses on international conflict and globalization and advised geography undergraduate students. She subsequently served as the scholarships coordinator in the National and International Scholarships Program at Illinois. Bernazzoli received her bachelor's in international politics from the Pennsylvania State University and her master's and PhD in geography from the University of Illinois. She previously spent nine years in the Army National Guard and served in the NATO Kosovo Force peacekeeping mission in Kosovo.

Kurt Davies is the director of global awards at New York University. In this role, he oversees the outreach, advising, and nomination processes for fellowships including Fulbright, Truman, Marshall, Mitchell, and Rhodes. Before New York University, Davies served as the director of prestigious scholarships at James Madison University, and he has worked in the Center for Undergraduate Research and Fellowships at Villanova University and the Alliance for Higher Education and Democracy at the University of Pennsylvania. Davies is currently on the board of directors for NAFA. After a career as a travel agent, he returned to college as a nontraditional student, receiving a bachelor's degree in linguistics and anthropology from the University of North Carolina and a master's in higher education from the University of Pennsylvania. He received a Fulbright grant in 2010 to research post-Soviet language policy in Kyrgyzstan and is currently pursuing a doctorate in higher education administration at New York University.

Matthew Klopfenstein is the assistant director of national fellowships at the University of South Carolina, where he has been since 2021. Before this he earned a PhD in history from the University of Illinois, where his research was supported by fellowships from the Department of Education (Foreign Language and Area Studies), the Fulbright US Student Program, and the Association for Slavic, East European, and Eurasian Studies. From 2010 to 2014 he taught history and social studies at an international school in St. Petersburg, Russia.

Gregory A. Llacer is founding director of the Harvard College
Office of Undergraduate Research and Fellowships. An associate
of Leverett House and a former longtime member of the Harvard
College Board of Freshman Advisers, Llacer also has been the direc-
tor of the Harvard College Program for Research in Science and
Engineering since its inception in 2005. In addition to his Harvard
responsibilities, Llacer is editorial chair of the national *Mellon Mays
Undergraduate Fellowship Journal*; director of the Global Program
Office for Amgen Scholars, a consortium of twenty-four international undergraduate summer research programs in biotechnol-
ogy; and consultant with the LCLO Group for the Association of
Southeast Asian Nations Future of Work Fellows Program. He is
the recipient of the 2023 Winston Churchill Foundation Advisor
Award. Before his appointment as Office of Undergraduate Research
and Fellowships director, Llacer served in several administrative management roles in the Office of the President and Provost,
the Harvard College, and the Harvard-MIT Division of Health
Sciences and Technology. Before his arrival in Cambridge in 2004,
Llacer spent the first sixteen years of his administrative career at the
University of California, San Diego, lastly as senior research policy
analyst for the vice chancellor of research. Llacer received an AB
degree from San Diego State University in liberal studies with an
emphasis on education and conducted postgraduate study at UC
San Diego and San Diego State University in language policy and
cross-cultural education.

Lucy Morrison is a professor of English at the University of
Nebraska at Omaha; she is also director of the University Honors
Program and the Office of National Scholarships and Fellowships
there. She has worked with highly creative and academically gifted
students for most of her academic career, enjoying the classrooms,
where teaching students and exploring ideas with them has fueled
her interests in ensuring their educational possibilities expand.
Morrison's research interests lie in British Romantic literature, as
her coeditorship of the *European Romantic Review* attests. She has a
master of science in urban studies and another in criminology, and

she crosses disciplinary boundaries accordingly in her research and teaching interests.

Elizabeth Rotolo currently serves as the associate director of academic fellowships at Brandeis University. Before this role, Rotolo worked with gifted high school students at the Institute for Educational Advancement and residential college students at UCLA and Boston College. She started at Brandeis in September 2013, managing two cohort-based fellowships that provided programming, service, research, and leadership opportunities for undergraduate students, and has since transitioned into a full-time national fellowships advising role. She has published in higher education blogs and newsletters on the topics of holistic advising, team training, and job transitions and also enjoys facilitating conversations on meaningful self-care practices. She holds a bachelor's degree in psychology from Occidental College and a master's in education from UCLA.

Catherine Salgado is a Fulbright alumna who holds degrees in creative writing, applied linguistics, and Portuguese. She currently serves as a fellowships advisor at Arizona State University while pursuing her PhD in writing, rhetoric, and literacies. In this dual role, she provides writing guidance to undergraduates as they navigate international opportunities, including the Fulbright US Student Program and German Academic Exchange Service (DAAD) Research Internships in Science and Engineering. Her research focuses on building community-university partnerships and the role of storytelling in identity formation, meaning creation, and belonging.

Meredith Raucher Sisson is the associate director of Virginia Commonwealth University's National Scholarship Office (NSO), where she supports undergraduates, graduate students, and alumni in exploring and applying for national and international scholarships. She plays a leading role in developing the resources and programming in the office and teaches workshops and for-credit courses as well. Before joining the NSO, she worked as a fellowships advisor in the National Fellowships Program at Johns Hopkins University. She earned her PhD in the history of art from Johns Hopkins as well, after holding a predoctoral fellowship from the Gerda Henkel Stiftung in Rome, Italy. She has also presented and published her research.

Gwen Volmar is the director of nationally competitive scholarships at Duke University, where she works with undergraduates, alumni, and occasionally graduate students who are applying for scholarships and fellowships. Volmar started her career working in education research, nonprofits, and elementary school teaching. Her college studies included a yearlong study abroad and a focus on Spanish-language literature, culminating in a bachelor's from the University of California, Berkeley, in Spanish language and literature. Soon after, her advising career began at Harvard University, where she was first exposed to the world of fellowships advising and where she earned her master's degree in adolescent psychology. After fourteen years in wintry Boston, she is now enjoying the sunshine in North Carolina.

Karen Weber is the executive director for Duke University's Office of University Scholars and Fellows. In this role, she is charged with overseeing nationally competitive scholarships and merit scholarships for the campus. She has built a career on constructing, delivering, and assessing cocurricular programs for students. Before arriving at Duke, she worked for over fifteen years in honors education at the University of Houston and the University of Illinois Chicago, supporting students in applying for nationally competitive scholarships, among other roles throughout her tenure. Weber has a master of arts from the University of Illinois Chicago and a doctorate from the University of Houston in learning, design, and technology. Her research focuses on the benefits of experiential learning and electronic portfolios for students, faculty, staff, and employers.

Tara Yglesias has served as the deputy executive secretary of the Truman Foundation for the past seventeen years and has been involved in the selection of Truman Scholars since 2001. During this time, she has had the opportunity to study the trends and characteristics of each incoming class of scholars. She used this knowledge to assist in the development of new foundation programs and initiatives as well as the design of a new foundation website and online application system. An attorney by training (Emory University School of Law), she began her career by spending six years in the Office of the Public Defender in Fulton County, Georgia. She specialized in trial work and serious felonies but also assisted with the training of new attorneys. A former Truman Scholar from Pennsylvania, she also served as a senior scholar at Truman Scholars Leadership Week and the foundation's Public Service Law Conference before joining the foundation's staff.

advising on, 160, 164-65, 166-68; empathetic, 61–62; Fellowships Research Collective focus on, 9–10, 143–54; graduate student skill development in, 177, 181, 184; grant, 177, 184; Truman Scholarship policy proposal, 25–26, 29nn20–21

Yglesias, Tara, 5–6, 15